1994

Evaluating Marketing Strengths and Weaknesses

David Parmerlee

NTC Business Books

a division of *NTC Publishing Group* • Lincolnwood, Illinois USA

Library of Congress Cataloging-in-Publication Data

Parmerlee, David.
    AMA marketing toolbox. Evaluating Marketing Strengths and Weaknesses /
David Parmerlee.
      p. cm.
    Includes index.
    1. Marketing—Management—Data processing.
    I. Title.
    HF5415. 13.P3246 1992
    658.8'00285—dc20

92-14241
CIP

Published in conjunction with the American Marketing Association
250 South Wacker Drive, Chicago, Illinois, 60606.
Published by NTC Business Books, a division of NTC Publishing Group
4255 West Touhy Avenue, Lincolnwood (Chicago), Illinois 60646-1975, U.S.A.
Manufactured in the United States of America.

2 3 4 5 6 7 8 9 0 VP 9 8 7 6 5 4 3 2 1

*This book is dedicated to every young child
with learning disabilities.*

AMA Marketing Toolbox

Many marketing management books define marketing and provide terminology definitions. The *AMA Marketing Toolbox* has a different purpose. This series will guide you in collecting, analyzing, and articulating marketing data. Although there is some narrative that describes the components of marketing processes, these books define the relationships between the processes and explain how they all work together. The books also supply formats (or templates) to help you create sophisticated marketing documents from your data.

A SYSTEMATIC PROCESS . . .

Because markets change constantly and new marketing techniques appear all the time, a step-by-step system is needed to ensure accuracy. These books are process-based to allow you to be as thorough as possible in your marketing activities and document preparation.

. . . FOR PROFESSIONALS

Although these books are written with a "how-to" theme, they are written for marketers who have experience and who know marketing terminology and the objectives of the business function of marketing. The *AMA Marketing Toolbox* consists of the following books:

- *Identifying the Right Markets*
- *Selecting the Right Products and Services*
- *Evaluating Marketing Strengths and Weaknesses*
- *Developing Successful Marketing Strategies*
- *Preparing the Marketing Plan*

ROLE OF THE MARKETING ANALYSIS

How does the marketing analysis you will perform in these books fit in with other market planning processes? The marketing analysis tells a story about your marketing and reviews your strategies, objectives, and scheduling in view of budget considerations. It then helps you monitor marketing effectiveness. A marketing analysis can be tailored to any size company with any product or service.

The books in the *AMA Marketing Toolbox* series will help you go from data collection, to analysis, to planning and control, and eventually to implementation of marketing plans. The diagram below indicates where the books fit into this process.

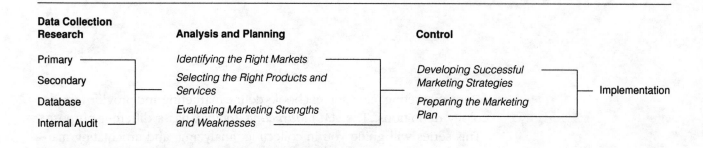

Data Collection Research

Primary

Secondary

Database

Internal Audit

Analysis and Planning

Identifying the Right Markets

Selecting the Right Products and Services

Evaluating Marketing Strengths and Weaknesses

Control

Developing Successful Marketing Strategies

Preparing the Marketing Plan

Implementation

Contents

Introduction

WHAT IS A MARKETING ANALYSIS?

A marketing analysis is an attempt to define, identify, and then evaluate the structure of the internal management of your marketing activities. Like its relatives, the market analysis and the product analysis, the marketing analysis's function is to apply research data and information that have been collected (via a marketing audit), analyze it, and place it in document form to give a detailed, accurate, and unbiased meaning.

The marketing analysis gives you a clearer understanding in a set format of your marketing department. It includes assessing how effective you have been at setting and achieving sales, revenue, market share, and profitability goals. It examines your level of efficiency in the marketing of your products to the marketplace by the activities you have used, the cost of marketing, and the control procedures you have utilized regarding your marketing operations and organization.

WHY PERFORM A MARKETING ANALYSIS?

The purpose of a marketing analysis is to identify and define the internal environment in which you operate. This builds a foundation for understanding the elements that affect the way you run your marketing operations. The key to performing the marketing analysis is that you must be as objective as possible. You should examine how your marketing operations are performed, with little or no interpretation. The analysis should mention the market and products or services only as reference points; to do otherwise could result in conclusions slanted toward your marketing actions, thus giving you an inaccurate picture of your marketing management and defeating the purpose of the exercise. The market analysis (where you will be marketing) and the product analysis (what you will be marketing) should have already been completed. The marketing analysis (how you will be marketing your products to the market) will link the market analysis and the product analysis together to give you a total picture of where you stand.

THE ROLE OF THE MARKETING ANALYSIS

The marketing analysis tells a story about the marketing of your product offerings to the marketplace. It explains what, why, how, when, and where events and activities happen. The marketing analysis tells you if your sales and revenue forecasting have been accurate and whether they have produced sufficient growth to cover your costs and generate suitable financial earnings. It also measures how you are approaching your marketing efforts. A marketing analysis should be performed every three to five years on the average. If your products have a short life span (e.g., high-tech products) and you are constantly introducing and terminating products, a marketing analysis should probably be performed each year. The marketing analysis is the first section in a strategic marketing plan, which is performed every three to five years, compared with a marketing plan, which is performed every year.

If yours is a new business, a marketing analysis would not be appropriate; a business plan would be a possible alternative. A business plan contains three basic marketing segments: a marketing plan, a product and service profile, and a market analysis.

WHAT IF YOU ARE PREPARING A SEPARATE MARKETING ANALYSIS?

The marketing analysis, as stated earlier, is usually part of an overall mar-keting plan. However, if you are preparing a marketing analysis as an independent document, it should include the following elements:

1. Title page or cover page

2. Table of contents

3. Executive summary (including the purpose of the analysis and its major findings)

4. Methodology

5. Limitations

6. Marketing analysis (body of report)

7. Exhibits

HOW SHOULD THIS BOOK BE USED?

This book provides you with a set of 77 marketing analysis formats to help you prepare a document in which data can be presented in an organized fashion. Part 1 (Data Analysis) explains and demonstrates the use of the formats; Part 2 (Data Reporting: Formats) includes the blank formats themselves. Before selecting and completing the formats, you will need to complete several other processes. First you will identify your marketing strategies. Next you will determine the effectiveness of your marketing activities including product management, pricing, distribution, sales management, advertising, promotion, public relations, and legal strategies. You will then work on monitoring and scheduling your marketing activities. Finally, you will learn to implement controls on your marketing.

Throughout this book, you will be alerted to many possible adjustments you may need to make in the marketing analysis. To conserve space, each format shows a limited number of lines for products, whereas your firm may have fewer or many more products to consider. Another example of possible adjustments to be made is the format calling for sales of a product for the past three years. If your product is new, you will have no sales to date, making the current market share analysis impossible.

The processes and formats in this book are designed for a consumer market, such as consumer packaged goods or retail service outlets. Firms in special markets, such as not-for-profit organizations or institutions, can adapt the marketing analysis to their own market's needs, problems, and opportunities.

Part 1

Data Analysis

The five units in this book are designed to lead you through a step-by-step process of organizing data about your marketing activities in order to create a marketing evaluation document. Before using the formats in this book, you will need to have collected, processed, and tabulated data relevant to your particular activities. The formats in the book will help you use that data to create a clear, understandable document to direct and shape your marketing efforts.

Your goal with the marketing analysis is to evaluate how you promote, sell, deliver, service, monitor, protect, and develop products. But the bottom line is to determine how you can maintain or increase revenues. You need to look at how you can save money by becoming more efficient in your marketing activities to get more "bang for the buck." You also need to look at how you can make money by uncovering new opportunities.

Unit 1

Identifying Your Marketing Management Objectives and Strategies

This unit establishes your current objectives and strategies and measures where you stand in meeting your marketing objectives. The purpose is to determine what your beliefs and predictions are in regard to generating sales, obtaining profitability, and controlling your market position. Remember that you are evaluating your *current* forecasts and projections based on your marketing situation. You are not interpreting those changes but rather establishing where you are going based on your present marketing actions.

HOW ARE YOUR SALES AND REVENUES MEASURED?

The first step is to define how your current sales forecasts are established; that is, what is the basis for these estimates? Next, you should determine your sales and revenue forecasts over the past three years and the next three years. You should base your sales forecast on market potential, competition, production capacity, market trends, market financial health, your product's profitability, and your marketing activities and distribution processes. In evaluating your estimates, you should employ some verification measure to determine the validity of the numbers. You must be as objective as possible in a subjective environment to ensure the accuracy and value of the estimates. Ask your-self the following questions:

Quantitative verification.
- Are your numbers time specific?
- Are your numbers measurable?
- Can you track your numbers by product, by customer, by sales, by territory, and by store outlet?

Qualitative verification.
- Are your numbers realistic?
- Are your numbers financially sound?
- Do the numbers reflect seasonal fluctuation?

Do your numbers stand up to these tests? Your answers should be challenging and attainable.

Forecasting Sales

In analyzing your currently expected sales performance, you need to look at your sales from many different aspects. You should look at each product on its own, at total sales compared with sales potential, and at sales related to generating revenues. Although only one format is provided here, some marketers like to look at their sales forecast through the "product analysis–product performance" categories (i.e., by customer type).

The following formats provide a method of reviewing your past and present sales forecasts. First, you demonstrate how you arrived at your sales forecasts and then show your actual sales figures. Once you have completed that part of the analysis, you will compare the actual sales with sales forecasts in order to determine how accurate you are at predicting the future and how stable your sales volume activity is.

Format 1 helps you evaluate how effective you were at obtaining your sales goals. The first half of the format reflects the last three years. This is not a record of your actual sales; this is what you predicted your sales would be compared to what the actual sales were. The second half of Format 1 reflects the next three years. This is just to verify what your current predictions are for sales for the next three years. It is meant to be a sales forecast, not actual sales.

Format 1

Sales Forecast ($ thousands)

		19 — $	19 — Units	19 — $	19 — Units	Rate of Growth (%)	19 — $	19 — Units	Rate of Growth (%)
Product:	*Regular*	$405,000	675	$534,000	890	32	$646,200	1,077	21
Product:	*Large*	70,785	65	92,565	85	32	112,167	103	21
Total		475,785	740	626,565	975	32	758,367	1,180	21

Measuring Sales Potential

The purpose of recording sales potential in Format 2 is to establish the maximum dollar and/or unit amount of product line your company is capable of supporting (selling, servicing, etc.). This is based primarily on your capability to produce product and your marketing capacity (ability to sell, distribute, and service customers) for a year. The purpose of recording a sales forecast is to predict estimated dollar and/or unit sales of your product line for the year. The sales forecast comes from the sales and revenue forecast you established in Format 1.

The following format provides a method of recording your sales forecasts as compared to your sales potential. Your objective is to determine how you formulate your sales potential and if it is accurately predicting your sales generation limitations.

Format 2 evaluates how effective you were at establishing your sales limitations. The first half of the format reflects the last three years. This is not a record of your actual sales potential; this is what you predicted your sales potential would be compared to what the actual sales were. The second half of Format 2 reflects the next three years. This is just to verify what your current predictions are for sales potential for the next three years. It is meant to be a sales potential, not actual sales.

To determine your percentage of growth, subtract the previous year's unit total from the following year (i.e., subtract 1979 from 1980), then divide that amount by the previous year total (i.e., 1979 total). This will establish a positive or negative growth rate. The total line at the bottom of each format represents average growth rates of the overall product line.

Format 2

Sales Forecast and Sales Potential ($ thousands)

		19 __ $	19 __ Units	19 __ $	19 __ Units	Rate of Growth (%)	19 __ $	19 __ Units	Rate of Growth (%)
Sales Potential									
Product:	Regular	$605,000	1,008	$650,000	1,080	7	$700,000	1,165	8
Product:	Large	80,000	75	100,000	90	20	150,000	140	56
Total		685,000	1,083	750,000	1,170	8	850,000	1,305	12
Sales Forecast									
Product:	Regular	$405,000	675	$534,000	890	32	$646,200	1,077	21
Product:	Large	70,785	65	92,565	85	32	112,167	103	21
Total		475,785	740	626,565	975	32	758,367	1,180	21

Format 2 demonstrates a problem. Your sales volume is outpacing your ability to handle these sales in your regular products and your overall/total product line.

Projecting Your Revenues

In order to define your current profitability projections, you need to determine the revenues that will be generated as a result of your sales forecasting activities. You need to translate your sales expectations into earnings. Each year you need to make more money to cover rising costs or to reinvest into the company. You can do this by lowering costs, selling more products, or raising the product's price. Your product profitability statement will include product costs that are determined in the product development or product management section by your accountant or financial manager.

You should define your profitability projections by individual product and overall product line. The first half of Format 3 reflects the last three years. This helps you evaluate how effective you were at obtaining your revenue projections. This is not a record of your actual revenues generated; this is what you predicted your revenue levels would be compared to what the actual revenue was. The second half of the format reflects the next three years. This is just to verify what your current predictions are for revenues for the next three years. It is meant to be expected revenues generated, not actual revenue obtained.

Note that sales dollars are figured using the base unit price. If volume discount pricing is used your revenue figures may need to be adjusted.

Format 3

Revenue Projections ($ thousands)

Overall:	19—— $	Units	Rate of Growth (%)	19—— $	Units	Rate of Growth (%)	19—— $	Units	Rate of Growth (%)
Sales ($)	$475,785			626,526			758,367		
Sales (Units)	740			975			1,180		
Rate of growth (%)	N/A			32			21		
Costs of goods sold	$209,300			303,160			404,042		
Gross profit	$266,485			323,366			354,325		
Gross margin	56%			52%			47%		

Format 3 (Cont'd)

Revenue Projections ($ thousands)

Product:	19 — $	Units	Rate of Growth (%)	19 — $	Units	Rate of Growth (%)	19 — $	Units	Rate of Growth (%)
Sales ($)									
Sales (Units)									
Rate of growth (%)									
Costs of goods sold									
Gross profit									
Gross margin									

By product model
for each product

HOW LARGE IS YOUR MARKET SHARE?

The purpose of market share is to measure your "piece of the pie." This will help you plan growth and determine overall sales performance compared to the market and your competition. The first thing you need to determine is the basis for forming your market share estimates, which include the direction and speed of growth you will be experiencing in market share. (That is, are you growing or declining, and at what speed?) Once again, you need to demonstrate this by target market, overall product line, and individual product.

The following exercises provide you two methods to determine your perceived market share. Your goal is to establish a share level that reflects your presence in the marketplace. Remember that you are analyzing what you *believe* to be your market share based on your sales performance. The market analysis is the official word on what your actual market share status really is. Therefore, you determine what you believe to be your market share and then compare that data with market share analysis information to accurately identify your market status.

Market Share Relative to the Market Potential

In establishing your current market share projections, you need to analyze your market share using two methods. The first method is by market share relative to the marketplace. This method will determine market share as it compares to the market itself. This can indicate your level of potential growth. This growth will come from obtaining a new portion of the market or from taking away from part of a competitor's share. An example of a good market share estimate relative to the market would be in the range of .05 to 1.00 percent. The first half of Format 4 reflects the last three years. This format helps you evaluate how effective you were at predicting your market share. This is not a record of your actual market share reported; this is what you predicted your market share levels would be compared to what the actual market share levels were. Remember that market share is figured based on units, not sales. The second half of the format reflects the next three years. This is just to verify what your current market share predictions are for the next three years. It is meant to be what you believe your market share levels will be, not actual market share obtained.

To complete the format you will need to know your market potential. This information is located in the market analysis section, Market Size. If you don't have that analysis when you complete this format, you will need to establish on your own the maximum level of units that can be sold in the marketplace by you or your competitors. You can then divide your sales forecast into the market potential to arrive at your market share level. A sample calculation is shown here:

$$\frac{\text{Market potential:} \quad 1{,}000{,}000 \text{ units}}{\text{Sales forecast:} \quad 500 \text{ units}} = \text{Market Share: } 0.05\%$$

The overall amounts on this format represent market share for the entire product line.

Format 4

Market Share Assessment Relative to the Market ($ thousands)

	19 —— Units	Rate of Growth (%)	19 —— Units	Rate of Growth (%)	19 —— Units	Rate of Growth (%)
Market share (Units)						
Market share (Relative to market)						
Overall:	0.07	—	0.08	14	0.05	25
Product:	0.01	—	0.02	100	0.03	50
Product:	0.06	—	0.06	0	0.07	17

Market Share Relative to the Competition

The other commonly used method for assessing market share is rating your market share relative to the competition. This method is more popular simply be-cause your numbers will appear larger. The only problem with using this method is that it does not tell you how much of the market is available for expansion. A typical market share estimate relative to the competition (direct, indirect, or alternatives) for a company's products that are con-sidered to be major players in the marketplace would be 10.00 to 35.00 percent.

The first half of Format 5 reflects the last three years. This exercise evaluates how effective you were at predicting your market share. This is not a record of your actual market share reported; this is what you predicted your market share levels would be compared to what the actual market share levels were. Remember that market share is figured based on units, not sales. The second half of the format reflects the next three years. This is just to verify what your current market share predictions are for the next three years. It is meant to be what you believe your market share levels will be, not actual market share obtained.

To complete the following format you need to know your market forecast. This information can be found in the market analysis section, Market Size. If you don't have that analysis when you complete this format, you will need to establish on your own the maximum level of units that should be sold by you or your competitors. An easy method for figuring these data is to total all sales you are aware of by yourself and your competitors. Once you have established your sales forecast, divide that amount by your market forecast to arrive at your market share. A sample calculation is shown on the next page.

Format 5

Market Share Assessment Relative to the Competition ($ thousands)

	19__ Units	Rate of Growth (%)	19__ Units	Rate of Growth (%)	19__ Units	Rate of Growth (%)
Market share (Relative to competition)						
Overall:	30	—	35	17	40	14
Product:	20	—	20	0.00	25	25
Product:	10	—	15	50	15	0

Market forecast: 1,000 units
                     ——————— = Market share: 50%
Sales forecast: 500 units

The overall amounts on this format represent market share for the entire product line.

HOW EFFECTIVE IS YOUR MARKETING ORGANIZATION?

In analyzing your marketing situation, you need to understand your marketing "machine." Your marketing organization and the following marketing operations establish the way you run your marketing activities. Using the example of a marketing department, you need to address your personnel resources in terms of performing marketing projects, tasks, and duties. You need to determine the level of activity being handled by your current marketing staff. Is your staff qualified? Do they need more training or can they be trained? If they are not able to perform the marketing work, should they be reassigned or terminated?

Once you determine your staffing situation, how will you adjust? Will you expand, downsize, or change job responsibilities? What will be the results? How will you evaluate your decisions? The following concerns may apply to your situation:

1. Expansions to existing staff

   a. New hires

   b. Part-time/per project (e.g., outside marketing consultants)

2. Downsizing of existing staff

   a. Restructuring

   b. Shared job responsibilities

   c. Reassignments

3. Changes in existing staff's position responsibilities

   a. Promotions

   b. New position creations

   c. Job responsibilities (duties and reporting changes)

4. Effect on costs (direct, not marketing expenses)

   a. Compensation packages

   b. Training

   c. Other

5. Results of marketing staff plans (improvements)

ARE YOUR MARKETING OPERATIONS MONITORED PROPERLY?

The next step is analyzing your current marketing policies, procedures, and practices and evaluating how they interact with other departments and with the marketplace. It is very important that for every marketing action there are rules that govern how you handle marketing problems, needs, and changes.

Marketing Management Practices

In assessing your present operational program and consequently making changes, try not to burden your staff and yourself with a lot of internal marketing regulations. The goal is to recognize situations where you can employ some system of checks and balances for marketing applications, such as approval systems and processes to follow when approaching a marketing project. For each marketing project or process, you should have in place standard policies and procedures and a project control and approval system to monitor quality and ensure accuracy.

Information Collection and Reporting

If you do not have a fully integrated management information system (MIS) where marketing data can be input and extracted to monitor and measure marketing activities, you are behind the times and perhaps in trouble. An MIS is a marketing tool that gives you the ability to totally manage your marketing as well as your market and product affairs. You should also determine how your database system is configured and used. Database marketing is the method of the future, so the way you structure your marketing operations in relation to a database will be your key to success. In the consumer market, a typical MIS consists of a host database (single data source system) that is linked with the following areas:

- Database marketing systems
  - Linked to direct marketing efforts
  - Marketing analysis and reporting
- Sales generation systems (telemarketing, field sales, inside sales)
  - Survey and reporting
  - Forecasting and reporting (activity, pending business, etc.)
  - Data communications
- Order processing systems
  - Order entry reports (by sales source, product, customer, territory, and store outlet)
  - Accounts receivable reports (accounts receivable by customer, aged accounts receivable, invoices by customer, and customer's balance)
  - Shipping reports (shipping schedule and analysis by ship date)

- Inventory control reports (inventory pricing and reorder lists and reports)

- Fulfillment and follow-up transmittals

- Customer support systems (customer satisfaction)

  - Customer time tracking reports (support time, number of calls handled, and nature of calls)

  - Support time reporting (number of calls made and resolution time)

  - Problem reporting

If you are using an MIS system (manual or PC-based), your system should be configured to reflect the above areas.

Analyzing Internal Communications

Communications between parties within your company is a vital part of day-to-day operations. Misunderstandings about performing marketing activities inevitably occur; this section only addresses being aware of information, not creating good listening techniques. In analyzing your present internal communications practices, the main things to consider are control and consistency. Whatever you transmit, you need to maintain standard formats; this will easily alert you to a mistake or a miscommunication. Consider communications patterns over the last three years and the next three years within your marketing department, with other departments, with other business units, and with corporate headquarters.

HOW EFFECTIVE ARE YOUR BUSINESS EXPANSION ACTIVITIES?

Every business must grow and must have growth planning programs. Marketing plays a vital role in expanding a company. Most companies are constantly searching for avenues for expansion: new product lines, new customers, new business opportunities, and so on. You can achieve growth through internal or external means. *Internal* implies using existing re-sources; *external* implies depending on sources outside of the company. Consider the following business activities as implemented over the last three years and as projected for the next three years:

- Internal

  - New and existing products

  - Any changes

- External

  - Acquisition (new products from competitors)

  - Franchising

- Licensing (selling rights—all or limited)
- Business relationship alignment (e.g., joint venture)

WHAT IS YOUR MARKETPLACE STRATEGY?

Your marketplace strategy gives you insight on the market structure in which you are competing. Whether you interpret the market as mass or segmented, you need to establish and define your strategies for approaching the marketplace. The market analysis document provides you with market segmentation activities; here you are concerned with extracting your final market definitions and profiles. Although the term *target market* can refer to the simple identification of a trade area, the proper use of target marketing is selecting smaller and more limited market borders to better manage the area in which you will exist.

Identifying Your Customers by Product or Product Line

In defining your target market, you must first establish how you will select each market. The next step is to address the manner in which you defined your customer profiles in the target markets. Format 6 lists the attributes and variables used for target market selection and the target market definition parameters. Descriptors are those profile variables (demographic, socioeconomic, etc.) used to describe, define, and identify your target market and customers. The target market definitions are based on the attributes and variables used in the market segmentation model in the market analysis. You can use some or all of these variables to define your customer(s).

Format 6

Target Market/Customer Identification

Target Market

1		2	
Descriptors	Counts	Descriptors	Counts
a. *males*	*2,648,594*	*Males*	*9,846,575*
b. *age 20–24*	*4,446,509*	*Age 45–49*	*3,657,300*
c. *white*	*2,367,444*	*Hispanic*	*5,674,974*
(etc.)			
Total*	*345,346*		*234,562*

*Total represents cross-tabulations among descriptors, not total counts of descriptors.

Defining Your Market Niche

After you have analyzed your target market, you need to evaluate your current target strategy. This basically means that you state your niche within that target market.

HOW EFFECTIVE IS YOUR POSITIONING STRATEGY?

Positioning in this case means how you will place your products in the marketplace compared to other products offered by competitors and in line with customers' wants and needs. This definition is different from the term used in your product line definition; this activity is discussed in the marketing audit and also in the strategic marketing plan.

Selecting Positioning Criteria

To assess your present positioning objectives, make sure your target market parameters match the needs and wants of customers in the selected target markets. In understanding your positioning strategies, there are several variables you can select:

- Specific product features

- Specific product benefits (problem solving, need satisfaction, etc.)

- Specific product price attractiveness

Product Positioning Attributes

Your products can be positioned in the marketplace against other products currently or potentially there according to the following attributes:

- Differences (features, benefits, problems solved, etc.)

- Usage (who uses these products and why)

- Matching (target markets)

- Alternative methods

- Association

- Competition (pricing)

The following format allows you to record and evaluate your positioning strategy. You have already examined your customers' perceptions and preferences through the product and marketing analysis. Now you need to determine how you are positioning your products relative to the competition.

First, establish what attributes you will examine. Then rate your products and those of the competition based on those attributes. These ratings may come from data collected from your customers in previous market analyses, but now you will determine how *your* thoughts match those analyses. Select and place the attributes on the perceptual map model in the format. Label your products alphabetically: Product #1 = A, Product #2 = B, and so on.

Label competitors' products numerically: Competitor #1 = 1, Competitor #2 = 2, and so on. Now rank each attribute on the grid from 1 – 10 with 10 being the highest or most favorable rating.

Format 7

Product Positioning Attributes

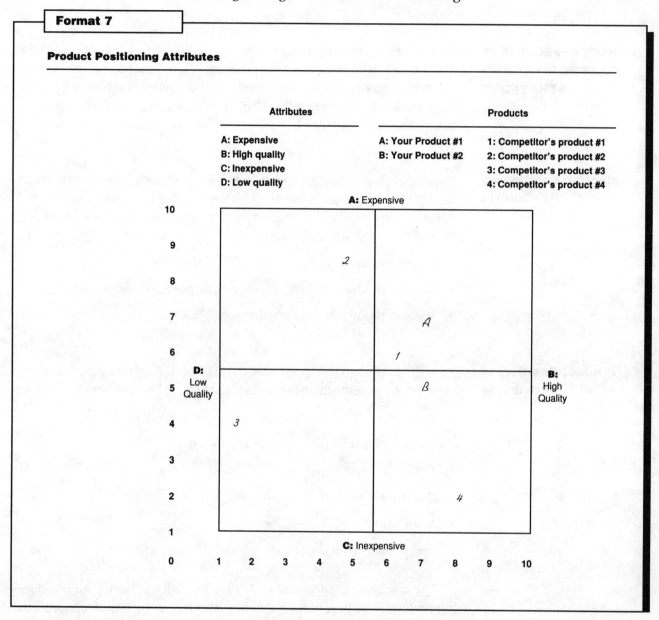

	Attributes	Products
	A: Expensive	A: Your Product #1	1: Competitor's product #1
	B: High quality	B: Your Product #2	2: Competitor's product #2
	C: Inexpensive		3: Competitor's product #3
	D: Low quality		4: Competitor's product #4

A: Expensive

D: Low Quality

B: High Quality

C: Inexpensive

HOW EFFECTIVE IS YOUR PENETRATION STRATEGY?

Penetration is translating market share goals into working strategies for your marketing functions. In measuring your penetration strategies, you need to determine your overall goals first. These goals are basically a restatement of your market share goals; however, these objectives are more qualitative, unlike the quantitative nature of the market share goals. You should ask yourself, for example, whether you are in the market for the long haul or you are just skimming the cream from the top. These goals should reflect the following methods.

- Long-term commitment
  - Increase your market share
  - Defend your market share
  - Control your market share and perhaps your competitor's share (Are you a leader or a follower?)
  - Maintain your market share (not losing or gaining ground)
- Short-term commitment
  - Increase your market share
  - Defend your market share
  - Control your market share and perhaps your competitor's share (Are you a leader or a follower?)
  - Maintain your market share (not losing or gaining ground)

The following format provides a method of viewing your penetration strategy by individual product and by product line. Record the actions you will undertake for both of the time commitments listed.

Format 8

Penetration Strategy Assessment

By Product	Short-Term Commitment	Long-Term Commitment
ABC	*Increase market share*	*Maintain market share*
ABC2	*Defend market share*	*Control market share*
By Overall Product Line	*Increase and defend*	*Maintain and control*

Unit 2

Marketing Function Activities

To this point, we have been dealing with overall strategies and forecasts. The marketing function activities deal with how you are getting your products to the marketplace. These activities are also called *marketing mix components*. These strategies should tell you how, when, who, and where you are implementing your marketing strategies. As you evaluate these tactics, they should reflect your overall strategies (target market, positioning, and penetration) and should link to your forecasts and projections.

All of the marketing functions should work together to fit in the overall marketing plan, but they should be programmed as individual plans to complement the other functional plans. The way this process analysis works for the marketing functions is that you go through each function and check off which activities apply. There is not much explanation, because each function's activities are self-explanatory. As a marketer, your job is to determine which activities you are currently using and then measure how effective and efficient your functions are.

As you go through each marketing mix plan, you will see sections that pertain to activities associated with each plan's action. Your objective is to go through each section and check off each item that describes your past, present, and future situations. As you are making your comments, remember to reflect on problems, problem solving, needs (changes), and positive and negative outcomes.

HOW EFFECTIVE IS YOUR RESEARCH PLAN?

So far the type of research that has been used in the collection of data to form decisions has been researching the market in which you will exist and the products you will offer in that place. Now research takes on a different role; here it is used to better understand the marketing functions. Marketing research in this situation is an ongoing business evaluation to monitor the marketing factors that could influence and change your marketing plan. It is here that customer satisfaction, advertising research, economic impact, sales, and product testing take place.

The marketing research process is probably the only marketing function that is more an art than a science; as a result, we provide examples of how you might approach collecting, tabulating, analyzing, and then applying marketing-related research.

In understanding your research activities at this level, you need to identify what types of research you have done in the past and what you are presently doing. You also need to understand results and whether they affected your marketing actions. You need to determine the following items: budget (Format 9), types of research performed (Format 10), types of research techniques used (Format 11), types of research methods used (Format 12), types of research instruments used (Format 13), and how the analysis and reporting procedures were handled (Format 14).

The following formats provide methods of evaluating how you have conducted your marketing activities. Complete each format for the last three years and the next three years by using the outlines provided.

Marketing Research Budget

The following format provides you a method of establishing what you have spent on marketing research, by product. Complete the format by placing the costs for each product in the columns and then totaling those amounts.

Format 9

Marketing Research Budget

Activity	19 _87_ Costs ($)	Percentage of Sales	19 _88_ Costs ($)	Percentage of Sales	19 _89_ Costs ($)	Percentage of Sales
ABC	10,000	5.0	11,000	6.0	5,000	4.0
ABC2	5,000	3.0	7,000	4.0	10,000	6.0
Total	15,000	8.0	18,000	10.0	15,000	10.0

Types of Research Used

The objective of this exercise is to establish what types of research projects you have undertaken. You need to identify research activities to assess their effects on individual products and the product line. Consider the following types of research over the past three years, and for the next three years:

1. Customer satisfaction

2. Product testing

3. Customer/market testing

4. Marketing mix/function testing (e.g., advertising tracking)

5. Other

Format 10

Types of Research Performed

19 *89*

By Product	Types of Research Performed	Results
ABC	Customer satisfaction to measure how well the product has performed.	Approved customer perception
ABC2	Sales promotion research to track the success of couponing.	Still collecting data
By Overall Product Line	Research has been conducted at a steady pace.	Improvements have been made as a result of research conducted.

Types of Research Techniques Used

The objective of this exercise is to establish what types of techniques you have used in conducting your research. You need to identify these activities to assess the effects on individual products and your product line. Consider the following research techniques over the last three and next three years:

1. Primary

2. Secondary

3. Internal database

4. Auditing

Format 11

Types of Research Techniques Used

19 *89*

By Product	Types of Research Techniques Used	Results
ABC	Primary	Will continue to use
ABC2	Primary and secondary	Same
By Overall Product Line	Primary and secondary	Same, but will investigate database

Types of Research Methods Used

The objective of this exercise is to establish what types of methods you have used to conduct your research. You need to identify these activities to assess their effects on your individual products and the product line. Consider the following methods used over the past three and next three years:

1. Qualitative

2. Quantitative

3. Statistical

4. Non-statistical (e.g., expert opinion)

Format 12

Types of Research Methods Used

19 *89*

By Product	Types of Research Methods Used	Results
ABC	*Quantitative Only*	*Data limited*
ABC2	*Qualitative and Quantitative*	*Good balance*
By Overall Product Line	*Both*	*Tried many different methods*

Types of Research Instruments Used

The objective of this exercise is to establish what types of research instruments you have used. You need to identify these activities to assess their effects on individual products, and your product line. Consider the following research instruments used over the past three and next three years:

1. Intercept (e.g., mall interviews) / one-on-one

2. Focus groups

3. Survey (mail or telephone)

4. Other

Format 13

Types of Research Instruments Used

19 _89_

By Product	Types of Research Instruments Used	Results
ABC	*Mall one-on-one interviews*	*Gave good insight to key issues*
ABC.2	*Same and focus groups*	*Same*
By Overall Product Line	*Used a mixture*	*Same*

Types of Tabulation and Analysis Used

The objective of this exercise is to establish what types of tabulation and analysis activities you used to understand your research data. You need to identify these activities to assess their effects on individual products and your product line. Consider the following forms of tabulation and analysis used over the past three and next three years:

1. Cross tabulation/summary tabulation (standard)

2. Statistical modeling analysis

3. Other

Format 14

Types of Tabulation and Analysis Used

19 _89_

By Product	Types of Tabulation and Analysis Used	Results
ABC	*Standard*	*Limited, but useful*
ABC.2	*Standard*	*Limited, but useful*
By Overall Product Line	*Standard*	*Limited, but useful*

Resulting Changes Made to Marketing Plans

The objective of this exercise is to establish how your marketing actions changed (if at all) as a result of research. The key is to show how the data affected your marketing plans. Consider the following types of changes to your marketing plans:

1. Impact analysis

2. Adjustment of marketing tactics (including all related strategies)

3. Impact on marketing research

Format 15

Changes Made to Marketing Plans

19 _89_

By Product	Effect on Marketing Plans	Results
ABC	Changed formula slightly to make it smell better	Changed advertising and sales increased.
ABC2	Waiting	Waiting
By Overall Product Line	Changes were small, but important.	Customers responded favorably to changes.

HOW EFFECTIVE IS YOUR PRODUCT MANAGEMENT AND DEVELOPMENT PLAN?

In the product analysis, you addressed the state of your product line and the markets to which it is targeted. This section is different, because it addresses how you are marketing your product line as it relates to the state of your product. Proper product management is a critical part of any marketing effort. Everything that has been discussed to this point is based on the performance of the company's product offerings.

The process of understanding your current product tactics begins with restating your portfolio strategy. In the product analysis, you were concerned with products as revenue sources and as structural entities. Now you are concerned with the products' image and identity as it relates to selling the product.

Most products and even services offer enhancement services (i.e., repair or support); these services should be established and then linked back into your profitability and revenues. Finally, you need to address any safeguards that are in place for controlling your costs to protect you from spending more than is budgeted.

The following format provides a method of recording past and current product developments. When complete, it will help you examine your success at managing product offerings. Fill in the format with information on each of your products.

Format 16

Product Development Budget

Activity	19 _87_ Costs ($)	Percentage of Sales	19 _88_ Costs ($)	Percentage of Sales	19 _89_ Costs ($)	Percentage of Sales
ABC Product update	20,000	2.0	—	0	—	0
ABC2 Product introduction	30,000	3.0	30,000	3.0	—	0
Total	50,000	5.0	30,000	3.0	—	0

Existing Product Line Strategy

In describing your existing product line strategy, consider the following issues over the last three years and the next three years:

- Cost reductions
- Product alterations
- Changes to marketing strategy
- Eliminations
- Price increases/decreases
- Volume increases/decreases

Use the following format to record the events that have had an impact on your product line strategy. This should include tactics you have used for individual products and the entire product line.

Format 17

Existing Product Line Strategy

By Product	Existing Product Line Strategies	Results
ABC	Altered product formula to make it smell better.	Sales increased by 5% within 6 months, remained steady
ABC2	No change	No change
By Overall Product Line	Modified products to reflect changes in consumer needs.	Enhanced product performance

New Product Line Strategy   Product introductions over the last three years and the next three years should be considered, both those developed in-house and those acquired.

Use the following format to record the events that have impacted your product line strategy by new product introductions and/or events.

Format 18

New Product Line Strategy

By Product	New Product Line Strategies	Results
ABC	Does not apply	Does not apply
ABC2	Developed through own R&D activities through analysis of ABC product's strengths & weaknesses.	No change
By Overall Product Line	Kept all new product efforts in house while considering competitors' acquisitions	Product changes were small

---

Product Mix Modification Strategy   The product mix over the last three years and the next three years should be considered, including modifications: additions, deletions, refinements, changes, and upgrades.

Use the following format to record the events that have impacted your product line strategy with regard to physical changes to your products or product line.

Format 19

Product Mix Modification Strategy

By Product	Product Mix Modification Strategies	Results
ABC	Does not apply	Does not apply
ABC2	Does not apply	Does not apply
By Overall Product Line	Planning to bring to market product ABC3 to eventually replace ABC.	Nothing to date

---

Branding Strategies   Branding strategies are those measures taken to develop product identity, product naming, and product image. Issues to be considered over the past three years and the next three years include the following:

- Brand developing
- Brand reinforcing

- Brand repositioning

- Modifications

Branding activities are vital to a product's existence in the consumer market because a product's identification and branding transmit a message to the customer: "Buy me!" Use the following format to record branding strategies that have affected your product line strategy.

Format 20

Branding Strategies

By Product	Branding Strategies	Results
ABC	Repositioned brand identity to reflect new formula that addresses "pine" smell trend.	Attracted new customers, sales improved 10% in one year
ABC.2	No changes	No changes
By Overall Product Line	Modified branding to meet the needs of customers seeking specific features	Products are better perceived as positive

---

Packaging Strategies

Format 21 considers packaging issues over the last three years and the next three years, including the following:

- Communication strategy (message)

- Usefulness of package

- Cost of packaging, shipping, and delivery

- Appearance of package at point of sale

In the consumer market, packaging is the physical extension of your branding. The package that surrounds, protects, or contains your product must convey your brand identity. Use Format 22 to record packaging tactics

---

Format 21

Packaging Strategies

By Product	Packaging Strategies	Results
ABC	Changes made on package to announce formula changes and explain the improvement.	Customers appreciated change
ABC.2	None	None
By Overall Product Line	Enhance current packaging to demonstrate product responsiveness to customer demands.	Overall, products benefitted in terms of value

you have used to enhance your overall product line and individual products.

Service Enhancements

Format 22 provides a place to consider additional revenue sources, such as maintenance, over the last three years and the next three years.

Service before, during, and after the sale of a product is very important. The service a customer receives is a value-added characteristic for your product. Use the following format to record service enhancements you have adopted to boost customer assistance for your product or product line.

Format 22

Service Enhancements

By Product	Service Enhancements	Results
ABC	New support line to help customers effectively use the product.	Callers expressed a few problems but enjoyed having a source for questions.
ABC.2	None	None
By Overall Product Line	Continue to offer value-added capabilities for product customers	Customers are more loyal to products due to support help.

HOW EFFECTIVE IS YOUR PRICING PLAN?

Although price is integrated into your product management, and usually there is very little cost associated with pricing, pricing should be analyzed separately because of its importance to every single marketing move. The pricing element establishes what it will take for a buyer to obtain your product.

Pricing strategies are simple in some respects, but in others they are complex. Your price must be high enough to cover your costs and generate enough profit margin to produce a steady stream of revenue. But pricing must be sensitive to the buyer. If the price is too high, the buyer will not buy; if it is too low, the buyer may not take the product seriously.

The actual costs are usually easy to determine, but linking actual costs to volume (number of units sold) or amortizing the up-front costs are subjective. The same is true of trying to determine what the customer will pay to obtain the product service you are offering. Once you can do these two things, you are ready to place a value on your product line offerings. It is this value that drives your sales and revenue forecasts and your profitability projections.

You need to see how your past and present pricing policies were set and how effective they were. You also need to look at your current pricing tactics and determine whether they are successful. Format 23 considers price as a function of your budget.

Format 23

Pricing Budget

Activity	19 — Costs ($)	Percentage of Sales	19 — Costs ($)	Percentage of Sales	19 — Costs ($)	Percentage of Sales
ABC	None	0	None	0	None	0
ABC2	None	0	None	0	None	0
Total	—	0	—	0	—	0

Pricing Formula Criteria

The criteria to be considered in Format 24 will help you establish your pricing formula. These criteria, to be traced over the last three years and the next three years, include the following:

- Cost (total: gross vs. net)
- Market demand (customer, competition, and product life cycle)

Cost can be defined on many levels and include many things. As a general rule, you can figure both gross and net prices based on cost, but primarily you work with net prices. Costs will help you determine the base price you need to charge. Market demand is more difficult to measure. While cost sets your floor (base), market demand sets your ceiling (maximum). You need to establish what the market will accept by looking at product research data, competitors' pricing programs, and the product life cycle. Use the following format to record your pricing criteria.

Format 24

Pricing Formula Criteria

By Product (per unit)	Base	Range	Maximum	19 —
ABC	$12.95	($7.05)	$20.00	
ABC2	$13.99	($5.96)	$19.95	
By Overall Product Line	$13.47	($6.51)	$19.98	

Setting Product Line Pricing Policies

In Format 25, you will consider the following items over the last three years and the next three years:

- Establish base price

- Discount policy (volume points)

- Special pricing (limited time)

- Price positioning (lower, higher, and same as the competition)

Once you have established the formula to figure your pricing levels, you need to define your pricing strategies. Determine what pricing variables you use in setting your price and selling your products. For example, do you structure your pricing to reflect volume discounting or special product features?.

Format 25

Price Strategies

By Product	Pricing Strategies	19___
ABC	*No discounts with the exception of lower prices used to sell inventory when the product is replaced.*	
ABC2	*Price set just slightly higher than ABC to reflect its higher grade.*	
By Overall Product Line	*Pricing very stable, not open to price wars and/or price changes.*	

Price/Cost Structure

The final component in establishing your price structure is to determine the level of profitability your pricing offers. The purpose of this exercise is to define the price you are using to move products and provide stable profits.

Use the following format to record various elements of your profitability. First record any discounts you offer. Often volume sales or quantity discounting is used. If you use these methods of discounting you will need to break them down as shown in the format. For example, sell one product—no discount; sell 2–5 products—five dollars off; and so on. Then record your base price, subtract the discount amount, and record your revenue level. Obtain your cost of goods sold from your controller or accountant and enter that amount in the format. Subtract your cost of goods sold from revenues to determine your profit level. Finally, divide your gross profit by your original base price to determine your gross profit margin.

Format 26 provides a place to establish your price/cost structure for each product and overall product line over the past three years and next three years:

- Volume (quantity discount for a unit volume sale)

- Price (list price per unit sold)

- Discount (amount discounted of a unit volume sale)

- Revenue (gross income generated from a unit sale)

- Gross costs (cost of goods sold by a unit sale)

- Gross profit (profit level of a unit sale, in dollars)

- Profit margin (profit level of a unit sale, as a percentage)

Format 26

Price/Cost Structure

19___	Product : *ABC*			Product: *ABC2*		
Volume (Units)	1–5	6–10	11+	1–5	6–10	11+
Price ($)	17.99	17.99	17.99	18.99	18.99	18.99
Discount ($)	0	1.00	2.00	.50	1.00	1.50
Revenue ($)	17.99	16.99	15.99	18.49	17.99	17.49
Gross costs ($)	7.00	6.50	6.00	8.00	8.00	7.50
Gross profit ($)	10.99	10.49	9.99	10.49	9.99	9.99
Gross margin (%)	61%	58%	56%	55%	53%	53%

Note: Price trends, costs sources, cost change (inflation)

HOW EFFECTIVE IS YOUR DISTRIBUTION PLAN?

The function of distribution used to be easy to define. Today the various delivery services, some linked by high-tech customer communications that can put products directly in the hands of customers, quickly and at low costs, have made selecting the proper distribution channels very complex. This situation is more critical in the consumer market than the industrial or business-to-business market.

In understanding your past and present distribution activities, you need to analyze the type of products or services you are offering and to what type of customers you are offering the products. Then you need to identify whether your strategies have been effective at getting your products to the customers. In evaluating your distribution strategies, you need to consider your coverage area, outlet types, timing, and direct or indirect (shipping) methods used. Format 27 helps you establish your distribution budget over the last three years and the next three years.

Format 27

Distribution Budget

Activity	19 —— Costs ($)	Percentage of Sales	19 —— Costs ($)	Percentage of Sales	19 —— Costs ($)	Percentage of Sales
ABC	15,000	1.5	15,000	1.5	16,000	1.6
ABC2	16,000	1.6	16,500	1.7	17,000	1.7
Total	31,000	3.1	31,500	3.2	33,000	3.3

Channel Selections

In outlining your distribution plan, you must establish delivery systems used to get your products to the outlet, then to the shelf, and eventually to the customer. These systems are called distribution channels and they can be used concurrently.

Format 28 provides a place for you to consider your selection of marketing channels over the last three years and the next three years. The channels might include any combination of the following:

- Dealers, wholesalers, and warehouse showrooms

- Franchising (franchise and franchiser agreement)

- Sell/ship delivery/direct (discount store, department store, specialty store, variety store, supermarket, catalog showroom, and convenience store)

- Joint venture (co-op arrangement, e.g., private labeling)

Format 28

Channel Selections

By Product	Channel Selections	19 ——
ABC	Shipped to retail specialty and department stores via distribution centers.	
ABC2	Shipped directly to retail stores and sold through select catalog vendors who receive product as ordered.	
By Overall Product Line	Products distributed through standard channels as well as special avenues, as needed.	

- Combined marketing efforts (advertising, direct marketing)
- Special (mail order, brokers, automatic/vending, door to door, and TV shopping)

Distribution Strategies

Once you have determined your distribution channels, you can establish control for each of them. You can establish things like how the channel is accessed and how the distributor will be used in the process. You can identify the role and importance of various players in the distribution process.

Format 29 is designed to help you establish your distribution strategies over the last three years and the next three years, including the following:

- System configurations
- Delivery programs (inventory control, shipping and handling, billing)
- Compensation packages (sales incentives only)

Format 29

Distribution Strategies

By Product	Distribution Strategies	19__
ABC	Shipped to distributors who then ship to retail outlets. Price incentives given if sold by a certain time.	
ABC2	Shipped to distributor and vendor to be delivered to outlets and direct to consumers.	
By Overall Product Line	Distribution performed by selecting the channels that deliver products in a timely fashion at low cost.	

Contracts Awarded and Status

Finally, identify your distribution methods by name and method of delivery. Who is transporting and delivering your products? How and when are their contracts awarded?

Format 30 will allow you to track your relations with outside firms, including the status of contracts with the following:

- Suppliers
- Shippers/transportation
- Warehousing
- Delivery (installations)

Format 30

Contracts Awarded and Status

By Product	Contracts Awarded	19 —
ABC	*Using combination of retailer's own distribution point and private sources such as AAA Transport for 3 years.*	
ABC2	*Using only private suppliers of distribution. Contracts awarded annually.*	
By Overall Product Line	*Current status of all distribution activities is favorable and active. It is our practice to use any distribution source that meets our needs.*	

HOW EFFECTIVE IS YOUR SALES MANAGEMENT PLAN?

The purpose of marketing is to get your product to your customer. Sales is the action that holds your marketing plan together. Although sales plays a key role in the success of your marketing plans, many businesses gear their marketing activities solely toward sales and salespeople. The trick is to balance sales with the other eight marketing functions to form a well-supported and integrated marketing plan.

When assessing your sales activities, you should identify who is selling your products. Then you need to evaluate the motivation of your sales force by means of sales incentives and compensation for their performance based on quota levels. Then you must determine how they will sell, what customers they will sell to, and where their sales area is located now (physical area or key accounts). Finally, you need to determine how they are being managed and what system is being used to monitor and track their performance. Format 31 will help you assess your sales budget over the last three years and the next three years.

Format 31

Sales Management Budget

Activity	19 — Costs ($)	Percentage of Sales	19 — Costs ($)	Percentage of Sales	19 — Costs ($)	Percentage of Sales
ABC	*20,000*	*2.0*	*22,000*	*2.2*	*22,000*	*2.2*
ABC2	*21,000*	*2.1*	*23,000*	*2.3*	*24,000*	*2.4*
Total*	*41,000*	*4.1*	*45,000*	*4.5*	*46,000*	*4.6*

*Total budget does *not* include salesperson's compensation.

Sales Force Activities

To evaluate your sales management, you must determine how you approach selling your product(s). Your objective is to determine which salespeople you use and why you choose them to sell your products. How are your salespeople used? What number of salespeople do you employ? How are they recruited and trained?

In the consumer market the salesperson's role is limited. In comparison, an industrial salesperson has a great deal to say about the final purchase. As a result, in either case it is important to evaluate how you select your salespeople and train them to sell. Depending on the size of your company and/or the size of your product line you may assign salespeople to only one or several products.

Format 32 provides a place for you to evaluate your sales force activities over the last three years and the next three years, including internal and independent representatives, the size of the sales force, recruitment activities, and training in selling skills and product knowledge.

Format 32

Sales Force Activities

By Product	Sales Force	19___
ABC	All internal, using 10 knowledgeable professionals located nationally.	
ABC2	Mixture of internal and external professionals with solid product knowledge.	
By Overall Product Line	Use both internal and external salespeople. Maintain a small yet solid team that knows the product and market.	

Internal Sales Promotions

Once you've identified who is selling your products, you can determine what will make them sell more. Sales promotions are generally a good way to provide this incentive. Remember that sales promotions for salespeople and for customers are two distinct things. And among salespeople, sales promotions and promotions are also different. The key to sale promotions for salespeople is that they are straightforward—based on money or some equivalent value-added reward such as a trip.

Incentives come in the form of regular compensation packages including bonus and commission, and/or special compensation systems such as winning a contest. You need to identify the types of incentives you are providing and whether they are sufficient. Remember, again, that incentives can be given across an entire product line or just for individual products.

In Format 33, you will consider the programs used to motivate the sales force over the last three years and the next three years, including volume incentives for salespeople and bonuses linked to sales volume.

Format 33

Internal Sales Promotions

By Product	Sales Promotions	19__
ABC	Incentives are based on annual bonuses given for sales over and above a certain level.	
ABC2	Special awards given for sales of this particular product.	
By Overall Product Line	It is our practice to focus on many broad sales promotions to sell product.	

Setting Sales Quota Plans and Compensation Programs

The next step in evaluating your sales management activities is to examine your compensation procedures. The first format in this section deals with quota levels upon which your compensation structures are based. The second format adapts the quota levels to individual salespersons' plans. Remember that quotas can be based on just about anything—from experience to geography to accounts served. Although individual product quotas can be used, this first model only deals with straight volume sales of total products sold. The second format is designed to accommodate compensation plans by product.

In Format 34, you will display quota levels and compensation plans in terms of units and dollar amounts for each salesperson. Compensation may be set in various plans, such as the following:

- Straight commission
- Draw against commission (base, pay-back, rate)
- Salary plus commission (base, rate-volume level)
- Salary plus commission (base, profit margin level)

Sales figures in the format are based on a single sale (volume of one) of both products.

Establishing Prospecting Methods

Next you will determine how your sales force approaches and obtains sales. The sales cycle can be unpredictable and unstable. The key is to establish how to direct your staff to generate sales. In the consumer market, with the exception of dealer or in-person outlets, a salesperson's role is already defined. Outlets are contracted and there is little direct contact with the person who actually purchases the product. In this situation, a salesperson needs to rate and rank stores that are most likely to move your product.

Format 34

Sales Quota and Compensation Plans

Salesperson	19 — $	19 — Units	19 — $	19 — Units	Rate of Growth (%)	19 — $	19 — Units	Rate of Growth (%)
F. Smith	200,000	10,000	300,000	15,000	50	300,000	15,000	0
J. Doe	400,000	20,000	500,000	25,000	-25	500,000	25,000	0
M. Jones	400,000	20,000	400,000	20,000	0	400,000	20,000	0
Total	1,000,000	50,000	1,200,000	60,000	0	1,200,000	60,000	0

Salesperson F. Smith

By Product	Compensation Programs	19 —
ABC	2% commission on product sold. Additional 1% bonus if quota is achieved.	
ABC2	None	
By Overall Product Line	$35,000 salary plus commission.	

Format 35 provides a place to evaluate your methods for identifying, qualifying, and prioritizing your potential customers for the last three years and the next three years.

Assigning Sales Areas for Territory Control

Controlling which salespeople work where and with whom is pivotal in sales generation. The goal of this exercise is to determine the effectiveness of how your territories are assigned to salespeople.

Format 35

Prospecting Methods

By Product	Prospecting Methods	19 —
ABC	Salespeople are instructed to push this product at AAA Department Stores.	
ABC2	Salespeople are instructed to deal with small stores to obtain shelf space and sell product.	
By Overall Product Line	In general, the sales force prioritizes stores that sell more product.	

In Format 36, you will evaluate sales area assignments for the last three years and the next three years, considering the following elements:

- Sales area configuration method (by salesperson, geographic area, customer density, or customer size)

- Lead generation (tracking) program used

- Key accounts (major customers)

Format 36

Territory Control Definition

By Product	Territory Assignment	Salesperson Assignment	19___
ABC	Based on key accounts	Based on knowledge of accounts	
ABC2	Based on geographic area	Based on knowledge of area	
By Overall Product Line	Mixture of geographic area and key customers	Knowledge is key in majority of sales territories	

Sales Activity Tracking

The final component to understanding your sales management is to focus on how a sale is created. In addition, you need to establish how to track and monitor sales results and turn them into actions. This information should be linked to individual salespeople.

Format 37 allows you to track sales activities by individual salespeople, covering the entire sales cycle: approach, interview, demonstration, proposal, and close. The elements to be considered over the last three years and the next three years include the following:

- Number of sales calls made per period

- Average number of sales calls per sale

- Average dollar size per sale and reorder

Format 37

Sales Activity Tracking

By Product	Sales Activity	19___
ABC	The normal sales cycle is usually very short (1-2 phone calls in in a 1-month period). Salespeople submit a monthly report.	
ABC2	Same as above.	
By Overall Product Line	The sales cycle is short due to knowledge of the customer. Salespeople are expected to make list of contacts and report to management their results.	

HOW EFFECTIVE IS YOUR ADVERTISING PLAN?

Everyone loves the communications side of the marketing plan because it is perceived as glamorous. Although you have more latitude with advertising, it should be structured with clearly set goals. There are three parts to marketing communications: advertising, promotion, and public relations. If sales is the "push," then advertising is the "pull." Advertising transmits your marketing message via several vehicles (medium) to your target audience (customers). This allows you to alert your potential customers to your product's benefits and features so they will want to make a purchase. In short, advertising enhances and supports your sales and distribution marketing efforts.

In understanding your advertising activities, you need to identify what types of messages you have used and what types of mediums you should use to communicate with your target audience. When you are assessing your advertising strategy, you need to keep in mind what type of advertising would best meet your needs: straight, cooperative, or trade. You also need to consider your objectives (methodology), such as what you have been trying to achieve, whom you have been trying to reach (audience/customer profile), when you have been trying to reach them (time period and one time vs. campaign series), where you have been trying to reach them (geographic coverage), how often you have been trying to reach them (frequency), and what types of media you have used. You also need to evaluate the creative and production staff who have been involved in preparing your advertising.

The formats in this section provide you methods of viewing how you conduct your advertising activities. Complete each format according to the outline and structure shown.

Setting the Advertising Budget

The advertising budget should take into account the last three years and the next three years, including creative costs, production costs, media costs, and any cooperative agreements.

Format 38

Advertising Budget

Activity	19 ___ Costs ($)	Percentage of Sales	19 ___ Costs ($)	Percentage of Sales	19 ___ Costs ($)	Percentage of Sales
ABC	20,000	1.0	25,000	2.5	25,000	2.5
ABC2	30,000	2.0	25,000	2.5	27,000	2.7
Total	50,000	3.0	50,000	5.0	52,000	5.2

Messages/Theme Strategies

The first thing you need to learn about your advertising is what you are conveying to your audience, the customers. The purpose of this exercise is to determine what message you are projecting.

Format 39 allows you to trace your message or theme strategies used over the last three years and the next three years, such as the following:

- Establish awareness
  - Informing
  - Persuading
  - Reminding
- Improve attitudes

Format 39

Message/Theme Strategies for Advertising

By Product	Messages/Themes Used	19 ——
ABC	Reinforce product's positives based on age.	
ABC2	Generate awareness of this new product by informing customers about it.	
By Overall Product Line	Make customers aware of product features and benefits.	

Creative Developments

Another element of advertising is creativity. Creating advertising is considered by many to be glamorous and unlimited. However, the true definition of marketing management involves establishing criteria or parameters for creative people to use when developing advertising.

Your objective in this exercise is to establish what types of creative activities you have employed and what limitations you used to make the advertising activities conform to your overall marketing approach.

Format 40 helps you establish the key elements or criteria for your creative developments over the last three years and the next three years, such as the following:

- Art and design developments
- Copy (content) developments
- Audio (music) developments
- Video/film developments

Format 40

Creative Developments for Advertising

By Product	Creative Developments	19 ——
ABC	*Primarily using print. Designs with heavy copy have been preferred. Logos and direct response (1-800) are used.*	
ABC2	*Focusing on radio and TV. Both audio and video used to interest the viewer.*	
By Overall Product Line	*All creative avenues are being used to generate interest and excitement.*	

Final Production Management

Once the creative portion of the advertising process has been approved it must be converted into the actual advertising act that is, in turn, regenerated in production. These actions form the final version of your communication to the audience. Your objective in this exercise is to establish what activities you use in translating art into action.

Format 41 allows you to track your production management decisions over the last three years and the next three years concerning such elements as layout and design activities, photography (stock or custom), typesetting, mechanicals (separations), and printer involvement.

Format 41

Final Production Management for Advertising

By Product	Production Management	19 ——
ABC	—	
ABC2	—	
By Overall Product Line	*All final production of advertising is handled through outside design firm, AAA Advertising. No problems.*	

Controlling the Legal Ramifications of Advertising Content

One of the key issues in business today is how your actions affect the market in which you exist and how you can protect yourself from any resulting legal problems. Unfortunately, your marketing acts can have a negative impact on your business because of certain legal ramifications.

There are many issues and laws about which you should be informed. Have an attorney work you to research the laws, rules, and regulations that could impact your marketing activities. Also, record any pending legal actions against your company. This should include lawsuits and violations, plus their predicted outcomes

Format 42 helps you track legal issues over the last three years and the next three years, including the following actions:

- Claim substantiation

- Unfair/deceptive messages

- Registered trademark location

- Guarantees/testimonials

- Use of re-released images

Format 42

Legal Ramifications of Advertising Content

By Product	Legal Ramifications	19——
ABC	Redesigned labeling to provide better customer warning information.	
ABC2	No legal problems	
By Overall Product Line	The product is always reviewed by our legal staff as a method of preventing problems.	

Media Strategies Used

One fundamental element of advertising is the message, the other is the medium used to transmit that message. *Medium* selection in this context defines where you bought advertising space and time. *Media* purchasing is the selection of a specific medium's vehicle for message transmission. For example, one *medium* is print. The *media* you may have chose to use from the print medium would be *USA Today, The Wall Street Journal,* or another daily newspaper.

In this section you will outline how you buy media by focusing on the following media strategies over the last three years and the next three years:

- Media factors

  - Gross rating points (GRP)

  - Cost per 1,000

  - Cost per sale

- Media demographics (relative to prospects)

- Media characteristics (relative to creative requirement

Format 43

Media Strategies for Advertising

By Product	Media Strategies	19 ——
ABC	*Using GRP, this product is advertised via local TV networks across the U.S.*	
ABC2	*Using cost per sale, this product is advertised in newspapers with coupons tied to a specific store for purchase.*	
By Overall Product Line	*Using the method of cost per exposure, all products are advertised in a consistent flow.*	

Medium Selections Used

The purpose of this section is to determine which mediums you have used to deliver your advertising message. This will help pinpoint where you are spending your advertising dollars. Using previous market research and information on the medium's specific media can help you determine which mediums offer you the most efficient and cost effective way of reaching your audience.

In Format 44, you will evaluate your media selections over the last three years and the next three years in local, regional, and national markets. You also should determine evaluation and buying criteria for each medium used:

- Direct marketing (mail, videocassette, phone, cable TV)

- Direct response/direct order (interactive TV, 800 or 900 numbers, business reply cards)

- Outdoor/general signage (billboard, transit, arena, window and door signs)

- Sports (note: promotion section)

- Television (cable and broadcast)

- Radio (spot)

- Print (newspaper, insert, FSI, brochure, magazine)

- Internal (corporate logo on letterhead and business cards)

- Movie and videotape inserts

- Specialty (posters, sales premiums, banners)

- Point of purchase (floor displays/stands, coupon dispensers, video grocery carts, shelf-talkers/danglers, counter/shelf units, and testers/sampling devices)

Format 44

Medium Selections for Advertising

By Product	Mediums Used	19___
ABC	Direct mail, cable and broadcast TV, newspapers, and point-of-purchase.	
ABC2	Same, plus magazine ads and FSIs.	
By Overall Product Line	Using a strong medium and media mix. Concentrate on direct marketing using databases.	

Advertising Response Tracking Results

The final part of a complete advertising program is to check how effective your advertising activities have been. This is generally part of your ongoing marketing research. Your goal is to assess what tracking activities you have used and what their results were.

Format 45 allows you to track customer recall of your advertising as well as its effect on purchases over the last three years and the next three years.

Format 45

Advertising Response Tracking Results

By Product	Advertising Response Tracking	19 ___
ABC	Tracked media efforts by selected sampling of viewers who watched TV commercials; was not effective.	
ABC2	No tracking.	
By Overall Product Line	As needed, response tracking is employed to establish the effectiveness of our advertising strategies.	

HOW EFFECTIVE IS YOUR PROMOTION PLAN?

Promotion is the second part of the marketing communications equation. The purpose of promotion is to support and enhance your advertising strategies. Promotion takes several forms; in this case, promotion is any marketing event, special value-added program, and the give-away or sale of secondary products designed to draw attention to your primary products. In the old days, promotions were just an extra way to promote your products. Today, promotion has a major impact on selling your products. Sales promotions in this context are unlike the sales promotions that exist in sales management, where sales incentives are set up to encourage salespeople to sell more products. In this environment, sales promotions are established to encourage customers to buy more products.

When looking at the ways you have been using promotion, you need to use the same methodology as for advertising; the difference lies in the type of media that are available.

Promotion Budget

Format 46 provides a space to establish your budget, including creative costs, production costs, and media costs, as well as any cooperative agreements.

Format 46

Promotion Budget

Activity	19 __ Costs ($)	Percentage of Sales	19 __ Costs ($)	Percentage of Sales	19 __ Costs ($)	Percentage of Sales
ABC	10,000	1.0	12,000	1.2	13,000	1.3
ABC2	8,000	.8	10,000	1.0	12,000	1.2
Total	18,000	1.8	22,000	2.2	25,000	2.5

Assessing Your Message/Theme Strategies

Format 47 helps you assess your promotion messages or themes over the last three years and the next three years. Promotional goals you should consider include the following:

- Establish awareness
  - Informing
  - Persuading
  - Reminding
- Improve attitudes

Format 47

Message/Theme Strategies for Promotion Activities

By Product	Message/Theme Used	19 __
ABC	Taking the advertising theme of reinforcement, this product message was used in trade shows.	
ABC2	Same as above, but also utilized couponing and sales promotions.	
By Overall Product Line	In general, trade shows and sales incentives reflected the same message used in advertising.	

Evaluating Creative Developments for Promotion Activities

As with advertising management, your goal is to establish parameters within which creative people can create promotion activities.

Format 48 will help you evaluate your creative developments over the last three years and the next three years. Developments to be considered include the following:

- Art and design
- Copy (content)
- Audio (music)
- Video/film

Format 48

Creative Developments for Promotion Activities

By Product	Creative Developments	19 ___
ABC	Art, audio, and video elements combined with great success for trade show exhibit.	
ABC2	Design for coupons including bar codes, was poor. Newer, cleaner sample needs to be created.	
By Overall Product Line	All creative developments have used many audio and video elements with great success.	

Final Production Management

Once the creative portion of the promotion process has been established it must be converted into the actual act that is, in turn, regenerated in production. These actions form the final version of your communication to the audience. Your objective is to establish what activities you use in translating art into action.

Format 49 will help you assess final production for promotions over the last three years and the next three years, including the following activities:

- Layout and design
- Photography (stock or custom)
- Typesetting
- Mechanicals (separations)
- Printer involvement

Format 49

Final Production Management for Promotion Activities

By Product	Production Management	19 ___
ABC	—	
ABC2	—	
By Overall Product Line	All final production of promotion materials is handled through our outside design firm—AAA Advertising. No problems.	

Monitoring the Legal Ramifications of Promotion Content

There are many laws, rules, and regulations you need to be aware of with regard to promotions. As noted before, you should have an attorney work with you to research these items. Use this information, plus what you have discovered through your market and product analyses, to complete this section. Also consider any pending legal actions against your company. This should include lawsuits and violations, plus their predicted outcomes.

Format 50 provides a place to track the legal issues regarding your promotions activities for the last three years and the next three years, including the following actions:

- Claim substantiation

- Unfair/deceptive messages

- Registered trademark location

- Guarantees/testimonials

- Use of re-released images

Format 50

Legal Ramifications of Promotion Activities

By Product	Legal Ramifications	19 ___
ABC	To protect our interests, we need to clearly place our logo on our trade show booth.	
ABC2	None	
By Overall Product Line	Minor problems only. All promotional activities are reviewed by our legal staff.	

Media Strategies Used

Your objective in this section is to determine which method you use to buy your media. Media buying, especially in the consumer market, deals with such things as merchandising and sales promotion.

Format 51 will help you assess your media strategies of the last three years and the next three years, including media demographics relative to prospects, media characteristics relative to creative requirements, media costs, and media availability.

Format 51

Media Strategies for Promotion Activities

By Product	Media Strategies	19 ——
ABC	—	
ABC2	—	
By Overall Product Line	*In summary, promotional media utilizes media characteristics and exposure.*	

Medium Selections Used

As we have already stated, selecting the proper media or mix of media is the key to promotional effectiveness. In this section you will determine which mediums you have used to communicate with your audience. This will help determine where you have committed your promotional dollars.

There are several ways of determining which mediums offer the most efficient and cost-effective methods of reaching your customers. Your prior market research on media usage and the medium's media can help you obtain this information.

Format 52 provides a place to evaluate your media selections over the last three years and the next three years for local, regional, and national markets as well as to establish evaluation and buying criteria:

- Promotion campaigns (sports, community projects, corporate)

- Sponsorship (corporate: event, place, individual)

- Merchandising (endorsements/licensing of name, catalog distribution, store assistance, displays)

- Sales promotions (external: product sampling, contests/sweepstakes/games, warranty card specials)

- Trade shows (show selection, display/exhibit creation, show management, transportation, lodging, booth space, results/inquiries)

- Price promotions (discounts, pre-priced shippers)

- Purchase incentives (rebates, consumer coupons, retailers' coupons, trading stamps, premium offers, money-back offers, cash refunds, value-added purchases, free gifts, bonus packs)

Format 52

Medium Selections for Promotion Activities

By Product	Medium Used	19___
ABC	Heavy merchandising, sales promotion (in store), trade shows, and purchase incentives.	
ABC2	Same.	
By Overall Product Line	Use of a strong mixture of all promotional activities.	

Promotions Response Tracking Results

The final part of a complete promotional program is tracking responses. This task is generally part of your ongoing marketing research function; however, you should at least be aware of your promotions actions and their results.

Format 53 allows you to assess the results of your promotion activities and their effect on purchases, such as the following:

- Coupon distribution and redemption
- General medium selection payback

Format 53

Promotions Response Tracking Results

By Product	Promotions Response Tracking	19___
ABC	—	
ABC2	—	
By Overall Product Line	No promotional activities conducted.	

HOW EFFECTIVE IS YOUR PUBLIC RELATIONS PLAN?

The final part of the communications side of marketing is public relations. This function interfaces with advertising and promotion. It allows you to take advantage of newsworthy events and activities that could promote your business's image.

In analyzing your past public relations activities, you use the same methodology that is used in advertising and promotions; the difference comes once again in the medium selection. In addition, special attention should be paid to your policies concerning media relations, your philosophy on community involvement, and your general publicity practices and public policy.

Establishing Your Public Relations Budget

Format 54 helps you establish your public relations budget for the last three years and the next three years, including creative costs, production costs, etc.

Format 54

Public Relations Budget

Activity	19 —— Costs ($)	Percentage of Sales	19 —— Costs ($)	Percentage of Sales	19 —— Costs ($)	Percentage of Sales
ABC	3,000	.3	2,000	.2	1,000	.1
ABC2	4,000	.4	2,000	.2	1,000	.1
Total	7,000	.7	4,000	.4	2,000	.2

Message/Theme Strategies

Format 55 allows you to trace your public relations message or theme strategies over the last three years and next three years. The public relations goals to consider include the following:

- Establish awareness
  - Informing
  - Persuading
  - Reminding
- Improve attitudes

Format 55

Message/Theme Strategies for Public Relations

By Product	Message/Theme Used	19 ___
ABC	*The message is different than the other section. This message has an attitude awareness to promote positive P.R.*	
ABC2	*Same as above.*	
By Overall Product Line	*In summary, the company and all its products have used methods to improve public perception.*	

Creative Developments for Public Relations

Public relations faces the same creative situation as advertising and promotions. In public relations, however, your goal is usually to take a different look at communicating to your customers. As a result, creative activity is normally restricted to thought and application.

Your goal in this section is to determine criteria for creative people to use in working on the public relations element. The purpose of this section is to establish what types of creative activities you have employed.

In Format 56, you will trace your creative developments over the last three years and the next three years. The following developments should be considered:

- Art and design

- Copy (content)

- Audio (music)

- Video/film

Format 56

Creative Developments for Public Relations

By Product	Creative Developments	19 ___
ABC	*No public relations activities besides press releases.*	
ABC2	*Same as above.*	
By Overall Product Line	*Public relations activities have been limited; however, when used, P.R. is effective.*	

Final Production Management

Once the creative portion of the public relations process has been approved it must be converted into the actual P.R. act that is, in turn, regenerated in production. These actions form the final version of your communication to the audience. Your objective in this exercise is to establish what activities you use in translating art into action.

Format 57 gives you space to record production decisions over the last three years and next three years, including the following activities:

- Layout and design

- Photography (stock or custom)

- Typesetting

- Mechanicals (separations)

- Printer involvement

Format 57

Final Production Management for Public Relations

By Product	Production Management	19 ——
ABC	—	
ABC.2	—	
By Overall Product Line	*Final production of all P.R. is handled through our outside design firm, AAA Advertising. No problems.*	

Assessing the Legal Ramifications of Public Relations

There are many issues and laws relating to public relations. Have an attorney work with you to research the laws, rules, and regulations that could impact your P.R. activities. Also, record any pending legal actions against your company. This should include lawsuits and violations, plus their predicted outcomes.

Format 58 allows you to monitor the legal issues regarding your public relations activities over the last three years and next three years. Legal actions to be considered include the following:

- Claim substantiation

- Unfair/deceptive messages

- Registered trademark location

- Guarantees/testimonials

- Use of re-released images

Format 58

Legal Ramifications of Public Relations

By Product	Legal Ramifications	19 ——
ABC	*None*	
ABC.2	*None*	
By Overall Product Line	*None*	

Media Strategies for Public Relations

Your objective in this section is to determine how you buy and/or place your media. Media buying and placement, especially in the consumer market, deals with methods from press releases to annual reports.

In Format 59, you will evaluate your media strategies over the last three years and the next three years, including media demographics relative to prospects, media characteristics relative to creative requirements, media costs, and media availability.

Format 59

Media Strategies for Public Relations

By Product	Media Strategies	19 ——
ABC	*Media characteristics*	
ABC.2	*Same*	
By Overall Product Line	*Same*	

Medium Selections Used

Selecting the proper media or media mix is key to public relations effectiveness. The purpose of this section is to determine which mediums you have used to deliver your message to the audience.

Format 60 allows you to evaluate your media selections over the last three years and next three years for local, regional, and national markets. You will also need to record evaluation and buying criteria for each media type:

- Press releases
- Seminars

- Open houses/networking parties

- Annual reports

- Public service announcements (PSAs)

- Article publishing

- Newsletters

- Book publishing

Format 60

Medium Selections for Public Relations

By Product	Medium Used	19___
ABC	Routine press releases discussing new uses for products.	
ABC2	Same as above.	
By Overall Product Line	Press releases are the only P.R. activities used.	

Media Relations Practices

The purpose of this exercise is to assess how well you work with the media and how reporters, journalists, etc. have helped or not helped you in obtaining positive media exposure.

In Format 61, you will assess your media relations practices over the last three years and next three years, such as the following:

- Media/press kits

- Incentives for favorable coverage (such as premiums)

- Establishing good/speedy communications

Format 61

Media Relations Practices

By Product	Media Relations	19___
ABC	—	
ABC2	—	
By Overall Product Line	Relied on personal relationships with contacts in media. They have been positive.	

Evaluating Your Community Involvement

Another public relations activity of special importance is getting your name out in the community. You need to devote an allotted amount of time to help local activities grow. Your objective in this exercise is to review your participation in the community and determine if it has had an impact on your product, either directly or indirectly.

Format 62 provides a place for you to evaluate community involvement, such as assisting with charity or arts events, over the last three years and next three years.

Format 62

Community Involvement

By Product	Community Involvement	19 ___
ABC	—	
ABC2	—	
By Overall Product Line	*Work with all Special Olympics groups in the Midwest.*	

Public Relations Response Tracking Results

The final step in a complete public relations program is to establish a method of checking the effectiveness of your publicity activities. This task is generally a part of your ongoing marketing research function.

In this exercise you will assess the public relations tracking activities you have used and examine their effectiveness.

In Format 63, you will monitor responses to your public relations efforts over the last three years and next three years, including their effect on purchases.

Format 63

Public Relations Response Tracking Results

By Product	Response Tracking	19 ___
ABC	*None*	
ABC2	*None*	
By Overall Product Line	*None*	

HOW EFFECTIVE IS YOUR LEGAL PLAN?

In any business activity, the legal ramifications should be considered. Changing Federal Trade Commission laws as well as the constant creation of and changes in other federal and state rules and regulations make it important for you to determine their impact on your marketing plan. It is important to make sure you are taking the necessary steps to protect and prevent any legal action from being lodged against you.

In identifying your past and present legal marketing activities, you need to confer with an attorney to be made aware of the latest legal actions that may affect your marketing activities. Your main concerns should be protecting your marketing actions from any legal exposure.

Legal Budget

Format 64 will help you monitor your legal costs over the last three years and the next three years.

Format 64

Legal Budget

Activity	19— Costs ($)	Percentage of Sales	19— Costs ($)	Percentage of Sales	19— Costs ($)	Percentage of Sales
ABC	5,000	.5	0	.0	3,000	.3
ABC2	2,000	.2	1,000	.1	0	0
Total	7,000	.7	1,000	.1	3,000	.3

Monitoring of Legal Activities

Throughout the communications portion of this marketing analysis (advertising, promotions, and public relations) we have discussed the legal ramifications of the processes. In this section you are concerned with marketing related legal and legislative forces that impact your ability to market products. Your goal is to identify how you monitor and react to legal forces.

Format 65 allows you to monitor legal activities over the last three years and the next three years, including the following issues:

• Product liability law changes and liability insurance costs

• Patent/copyright protection

• Lobbying/legislative activities

• Contract protection

Format 65

Monitoring of Legal Activities

By Product	Monitoring	19 —
ABC	Lobbying efforts to prevent federal laws regarding labeling from taking effect.	
ABC.2	Same.	
By Overall Product Line	Working with trade associations and private lobbying to monitor all legal activities. So far this has proven successful.	

Unit 3

Marketing Function Activities Scheduling

Once you have determined how you have been marketing your products to the marketplace, you need to see each function on a timetable format. This will aid you in evaluating how effective your marketing activities have been. There are two types of schedules to evaluate. One addresses the management of each function's activities (i.e., project manager), and the other is media placement schedules, which apply only to the three communications components of the marketing plan. Both types should be evaluated using criteria from the past three years and the next three years.

MARKETING ACTIVITIES TIMETABLE

This schedule determines when your marketing function projects began and when they ended. Each function should have listed the events and activities that transpired over the appropriate time period. Format 66 provides a place for you to monitor the timing and progress of your marketing activities.

MEDIA SCHEDULING AND BUYING

The placement of your media purchases is very important. How, when, where, who, and what are questions that need to be answered. The following formats are suggested for radio (Format 67), magazines (Format 68), cable and broadcast television (Format 69), outdoor advertising (Format 70), and newspapers (Format 71).

Format 66

Marketing Activities Timetable

19 ____	Start/Finish (Dates)	On Time (Yes/No)	On Budget (Yes/No)	Comments
Marketing research activities:				
Customer satisfaction	*6-91/12-91*	*Yes*	*Yes*	*—*
Media tracking	*6-91/10-91*	*Yes*	*No*	*Poor projection*
Product development activities:				
Pricing activities:				
Distribution activities:				
Sales activities:				
Advertising activities:				
Promotions activities:				
Public relations activities:				
Legal activities:				

Format 67

Radio Purchase Order

Client:

Product: *ABC*

Message: *Reminding customers of special sale*

Date Issued: *1-1-92*

Day	Time	Program	Seconds	From/To	Unit Cost	Frequency	Total Cost
M-F	*8 a.m.*	*News*	*30*	*Jan.-Feb.*	*$500*	*300,000 per day*	*$1,500*
"	*12 p.m.*	*"*	*"*	*"*	*"*	*"*	*"*
"	*5 p.m.*	*"*	*"*	*"*	*"*	*"*	*"*

Authorization: *S. Carr*

Accepted by: *M. Beesley*

Format 68

Magazine Placement Schedule

Product: **Begin Date:**   **End Date:**   **Date Approved:**   **Cost:**

Magazine	Jan.	Feb.	March	April	May	June	July	Aug.	Sept.	Oct.	Nov.	Dec.	Total

Name: *ATA Journal*

Circulation: 30,000

Closing date: *12-1-92*

Publishing frequency: *monthly*

Rate: *3 x 5, $995*

Number of exposures: 70,000

Contract time: *1 year*

1 *1 page*
2 *reminder*
3 *4-color*
4 *None*
5 *$995*

Total: $11,940

Product: **Begin Date:**   **End Date:**   **Date Approved:**   **Cost:**

Magazine	Jan.	Feb.	March	April	May	June	July	Aug.	Sept.	Oct.	Nov.	Dec.	Total

Name:

Circulation:

Closing Date:

Publishing frequency:

Rate:

Number of Exposures:

Contract time:

1
2
3
4
5

Total:

1: Page
2: Ad type (purpose)
3: Color/B&W
4: Issue/Theme
5: Cost (media placement and/or media placement commissions)

Authorization: *S. Carr*

Accepted by: *M. Beesley*

Format 69

Television Proposal

Product: *ABC*

Message: *Reminding customers of special sale*

Date Issued: *1-1-92*

Day	Time	Program	Seconds	Rating	HH (000)	From/To	Unit Cost	Frequency	Total Cost
Fri.	*8 p.m.*	*The Simpsons*	*30*	*10.0*	*500*	*Jan. only*	*$5,000*	*2 million*	*$20,000*

Authorization: *S. Carr*

Accepted by: *M. Beesley*

Format 70

Outdoor Proposal

Product: *ABC2*

Message: *Inform customers of improvements*

Date Issued: *5-1-92*

Position	Type	Year	Schedule	Unit Cost	No. Times	Total Cost
			Jan. Feb. March April May June July Aug. Sept. Oct. Nov. Dec.			
13th to Main	*Billboard*	*1*	x ——————— x	*$2,000*	*100,000*	*$16,000*

Authorization: *S. Carr*

Accepted by: *M. Beesley*

Format 71

Newspaper Proposal

Newspaper: *Times*

Product: *ABC to ABC2 (product line)*

Message: *Introduction (reinforcement)*

Issued: *1-1-92*

Day	Type/Day	Ad Size	Gross/Net	Date	Rate	Number of Inserts	Column Inches	Total Cost
M-F	*Morning*	*Full-page*	*$1,500*	*Jan.-March*	*X7*	*1*	*14 x 20*	*$10,500*

Authorization: *S. Carr*

Accepted by: *M. Beesley*

Unit 4

Marketing Budget

Determining how much it has cost you to market your products and services is a key part of marketing planning. Throughout the marketing planning process, costs and budgets should have been established. The formats in this unit allow you to add these amounts and display the results. They also allow you to check (using percentage of sales) to see if your marketing costs are in line with national averages. This system is not 100 percent foolproof, but it allows you to see if your numbers are realistic and efficient.

In evaluating where your marketing activities stand in terms of cost versus performance, you should assess each marketing function's budget, as well as your combined marketing efforts. Depending on where your products are in the product life cycle (determined in your product analysis), the cost of marketing will be high or low. The measuring tool used is percentage of sales; you will establish what percentage of a sale is devoted to a marketing expense. For example, if your sales are $100,000 and your cost of advertising is $20,000, your percentage of sales is 20 percent for advertising. The result will determine whether you are spending too much or not enough on your marketing expenses.

In Exhibit 4–1, guidelines are provided for analyzing sales volume and cost of marketing based on where a product exists in its product life cycle. As you evaluate your costs versus sales, you need to keep in mind not only the product life cycle, but also whether the costs are accurate and normal (false spending data) and if sales are under or over the sales norm (poor marketing habits). For example, you may discover that your total marketing expenditures come to an extremely high 60 percent of sales. However, this could be acceptable if your product is in the introduction stage, if the market in which you compete is costly, or if your sales have been low. This analysis is geared toward the consumer market; you should keep in mind that each market is different.

It is important to remember that these numbers are just guidelines; depending on your market, your numbers may be proportionately more or less. The final analysis of determining the proper amount of marketing costs should be averaged to reflect your overall product line. Also, these cost estimates do not include compensation (e.g., salaries) and operations expenses (e.g., a new MIS).

EXHIBIT 4–1
Sales Volume/Cost of Marketing Analysis

	Stage in Product Life Cycle			
	Introduction	Growth	Maturity	Decline
		Sales Volume		
	Low	High	Steady	Low
Marketing Mix Strategies				
Marketing research	6.0%	3.8%	5.0%	2.5%
Product development	3.0	5.0	6.5	1.5
Pricing	0.5	0.2	0.1	0.5
Distribution	5.5	7.0	8.0	2.0
Sales management	9.0	7.0	5.0	2.5
Advertising	8.0	9.0	5.5	2.0
Promotions	7.0	3.0	4.0	3.0
Public relations	2.5	0.5	0.5	0.1
Legal	4.0	1.0	0.1	0.1
Total (Actual Dollars)	45.5%	36.5%	34.7%	14.2%
Range (max.)	40-50%	30-40%	30-40%	10-20%
Total (Adjusted Dollars)	45.5%	12.0%	10%	5.0%

Totals in Exhibit 4-1 represent two indicators. Actual dollars are those being spent relative to a constant sales volume. Adjusted dollars are those being spent relative to the expected sales growth rates.

When evaluating marketing budgets, many people take the percentage of sales literally. In other words, they make the assumption that their marketing expenses will fall within these guidelines. This is very dangerous. The purpose of this exercise is to give you a system of checks and balances. The method of evaluating your marketing expenses is to go through each marketing function's budget, *then* use the percentage of sales process to make sure your numbers are realistic.

INDIVIDUAL MARKETING FUNCTIONS' EXPENSE REPORTS

Format 72 is devoted to listing each function's budget and marketing activity costs. You should be as detailed as possible to make sure you are including all related marketing expenses. This exercise allows you to view your entire marketing functional expenses.

Format 72

Individual Marketing Function's Expense Report

Activity	19 —— Costs ($)	Percentage of Sales	19 —— Costs ($)	Percentage of Sales	19 —— Costs ($)	Percentage of Sales
Marketing Research						
ABC	10,000	5.0	11,000	6.0	5,000	4.0
ABC2	5,000	3.0	7,000	4.0	10,000	6.0
Total	15,000	8.0	8,000	10.0	15,000	10.0
Product Development						
Total						
Pricing						
Total						
Distribution						
Total						

Format 72 (Cont'd)

Individual Marketing Function's Expense Report

Activity	19 —— Costs ($)	Percentage of Sales	19 —— Costs ($)	Percentage of Sales	19 —— Costs ($)	Percentage of Sales
Sales Management						
Total						
Advertising						
Total						
Promotions						
Total						
Public Relations						
Total						

Format 72 (Cont'd)

Individual Marketing Function's Expense Report

Activity	19—— Costs ($)	Percentage of Sales	19—— Costs ($)	Percentage of Sales	19—— Costs ($)	Percentage of Sales
Legal						
Total						
Total						

ARE YOUR OVERALL MARKETING ACTIVITIES EXPENSES ON TARGET?

These statements should include marketing costs only, not related expenses such as compensation for salespeople or distributors. The category of "Other Marketing Expenses" in the next format might include a new MIS system or database marketing system.

Marketing Function

Format 73 is devoted to listing each function's budget and marketing activity costs. You should be as detailed as possible to make sure you are including all related marketing expenses. By comparing cost increases with sales increases you will be able to analyze whether your sales growth is staying ahead of rising expenses.

Marketing Function and Product Statement

Format 74 looks at marketing costs as they relate to your products. This is a good way to identify which products cost you more to market than others.

Format 73

Marketing Function Statement

Activity	19—— Costs ($)	Rate of Growth (%)*	Rate of Cost (%)**	19—— Costs ($)	Rate of Growth (%)*	Rate of Cost (%)**	19—— Costs ($)	Rate of Growth (%)*	Rate of Cost (%)**
Marketing Research	15,000	—	—	18,000	32	20	25,000	21	39
Product Development									
Pricing									
Distribution									
Sales									
Advertising									
Promotion									
Public Relations									
Legal									
Total									
Percentage of Sales									
Other Marketing Expenses									
Total Marketing Budget									
Percentage of Sales									

* Rate of growth is the percentage of sales activity from your previous forecasts.

** Rate of costs is the percentage of marketing expenses, role of inflation, and/or rises in costs.

Format 74

Marketing Function and Product Statement

19——	Product *ABC*		Product *ABC2*		Overall	
	$	%	$	%	$	%
Marketing Research	10,000	5.0	5,000	3.0	15,000	8.0
Product Development						
Pricing						
Distribution						
Sales						
Advertising						
Promotion						
Public Relations						
Legal						
Total						
Percentage of Sales						

% = Percentage of sales

Unit 5

Marketing Control

In your marketing activities, you need to address your past and present control procedures to measure the effectiveness of these procedures. You need to see if the control procedures in place allow you to make adjustments based on changes in the marketplace, because no matter how well planned your marketing strategies are, marketplace variables, new information, and government regulations can all force you to alter your course.

In your past and present marketing control procedures, you need to evaluate your marketing management tracking systems, which should include checkpoints designed to adjust your marketing thinking.

MONITORING EFFECTIVENESS

The primary tools a marketer has available to monitor the marketing plan's performance are sales reports, marketing and media statements, and ongoing marketing audit results. Several of the trackings will require you to be knowledgeable in accounting; if you aren't, you need to work with your accountant or controller regarding marketing's role in the financial environment of your business.

Reporting and Tracking

Format 75 allows you to assess your monitoring activities over the last three years and the next three years.

Format 75

Marketing Plan Reporting and Tracking

Activity	Yes/No	Frequency	Results
Lead Tracking	No	No	None
Sales Reports Tracking	No	No	None
Order Taking/Processing Tracking	Yes	Monthly	Better record-keeping

Marketing Activity Tracking by Income Statement Analysis

This format allows you to view your marketing actions and see how they have impacted your overall financial health. You are provided an income statement that will need to be prepared with the help of your controller or accountant.

Format 76

Marketing Activity Tracking by Income Statement Analysis

Item:	19 ___ $	19 ___ Percentage	19 ___ $	19 ___ Percentage	19 ___ $	19 ___ Percentage
Gross sales						
Product A: * *ABC*	600,000	—	700,000	—	600,000	—
Product B: * *ABC2*	100,000	—	200,000	—	400,000	—
Total*						
Less returns/allowances						
Net sales	700,000	—	900,000	—	1,000,000	—
Cost of goods sold						
Beginning inventory						
Cost of goods purchased						
Total merchandise handled						
Ending inventory						
Total						
Gross profit*						
Gross profit margin*						
Marketing expenses						
Sales compensation						
Marketing functions*	100,000	14	150,000	17	300,000	30
Shipping	80,000	10	120,000	15	200,000	10
Payroll taxes and insurance						
Regional office expense						
Total						
General administrative expenses						
Executive salaries						
Clerical expense						
Payroll taxes and insurance						
Office expenses						
Depreciation						
Credit/collections						
Research/development costs						
Other expenses						
Total						
Total expenses						
Net profit						

* Numbers are produced by marketing management.

Note: Percentage represents percent of sales as it relates to costs.

UPDATING
As you track and monitor your marketing management performance, you need to be able to intercept your marketing strategies. This ability will allow you to make adjustments to your plan, alter strategies, and prepare for next year's marketing plan., Format 77 provides a place for you to map out secondary plans to be prepared if they become needed:

1. Marketing research adjustments

    a. Changes to marketing plan (strategies, projections, costs, etc.)

    b. New plan of action

2. Contingency planning

    a. Alternative strategies

    b. Benchmarks for safety valve

Format 77

Contingency Planning

Activity	Yes/No	Frequency	Results
Marketing Research Adjustments	*No*	—	—
Contingency Planning	*Yes*	*Quarterly*	*Adjust to customer attitudes/wants.*

PROVIDING SUPPORT MATERIALS
With every document you prepare, you need to include only the pertinent information. The reason is that if you include every single piece of data, your document would be so full of information that it would be difficult to read and understand. As a result, a support material section should be prepared for readers to consult for further verification of your marketing decisions.

Preparing the Exhibit Section
Developing the support material section begins with collecting and organizing the sources of information you are using, organizing the contacts you have made in collecting that information, and describing how the results of the information were produced. Then you need to make available examples of the data you obtained and used, such as actual research reports. Finally, you will provide the methodologies you used in producing the data estimates. Your objective is to compile the following information:

1. Information source, including each contact's name, address, and phone number.

2. Information (results) obtained.

3. Examples (actual raw data).

4. Methodologies used, including any processes, models, or formulas.

Part 2

Data Reporting: Formats

After you have input and processed the marketing data, the next step is to place that information in a format suitable for presentation. There is no need to include these exact formats in your final document; instead, a solid marketing analysis blends written narrative segments with matrix models and charts containing hard data. This breaks up the data being presented and gives the reader a sense of a beginning and an end.

Identifying Your Marketing Management Objectives and Strategies

Formats 1–8 should be used to help you establish your current marketing management objectives and strategies. See Unit 1 in Part 1 for explanations and examples of the formats.

Format 1

Sales Forecast ($ thousands)

Last Three Years

	19 ___		19 ___		Rate of Growth (%)	19 ___		Rate of Growth (%)
	$	Units	$	Units		$	Units	
Product:								
Product:								
Product:								
Product:								
Product:								
Product:								
Product:								
Product:								
Product:								
Product:								
Product:								
Product:								
Product:								
Product:								
Product:								
Total								

Format 1 (Continued)

Sales Forecast ($ thousands)

Next Three Years

	19 ___		19 ___		Rate of Growth (%)	19 ___		Rate of Growth (%)
	$	Units	$	Units		$	Units	
Product:								
Product:								
Product:								
Product:								
Product:								
Product:								
Product:								
Product:								
Product:								
Product:								
Product:								
Product:								
Product:								
Product:								
Product:								
Total								

Format 2

Sales Forecast and Sales Potential ($ thousands)

Last Three Years

	19 ___		19 ___		Rate of Growth (%)	19 ___		Rate of Growth (%)
	$	Units	$	Units		$	Units	
Sales Potential								
Product:								
Product:								
Product:								
Product:								
Product:								
Product:								
Total								

Sales Forecast								
Product:								
Product:								
Product:								
Product:								
Product:								
Product:								
Total								

Format 2 (Continued)

Sales Forecast and Sales Potential ($ thousands)

Next Three Years

	19 ___ $	Units	19 ___ $	Units	Rate of Growth (%)	19 ___ $	Units	Rate of Growth (%)
Sales Potential								
Product:								
Product:								
Product:								
Product:								
Product:								
Product:								
Total								
Sales Forceast								
Product:								
Product:								
Product:								
Product:								
Product:								
Product:								
Total								

Format 3

Revenue Projections ($ thousands)

Last Three Years

Overall:	19 ___ $	Units	Rate of Growth (%)	19 ___ $	Units	Rate of Growth (%)	19 ___ $	Units	Rate of Growth (%)
Sales ($)									
Sales (Units)									
Rate of growth (%)									
Costs of goods sold									
Gross profit									
Gross margin									

Format 3 (Continued)

Revenue Projections ($ thousands)

Product:	19 —— $	Units	Rate of Growth (%)	19 —— $	Units	Rate of Growth (%)	19 —— $	Units	Rate of Growth (%)
Sales ($)									
Sales (Units)									
Rate of growth (%)									
Costs of goods sold									
Gross profit									
Gross margin									
By product model for each product									

Format 3 (Continued)

Revenue Projections ($ thousands)

Next Three Years

Overall:	19 ___ $	Units	Rate of Growth (%)	19 ___ $	Units	Rate of Growth (%)	19 ___ $	Units	Rate of Growth (%)
Sales ($)									
Sales (Units)									
Rate of growth (%)									
Costs of goods sold									
Gross profit									
Gross margin									

Format 3 (Continued)

Revenue Projections ($ thousands)

Product:	19 — $	19 — Units	Rate of Growth (%)	19 — $	19 — Units	Rate of Growth (%)	19 — $	19 — Units	Rate of Growth (%)
Sales ($)									
Sales (Units)									
Rate of growth (%)									
Costs of goods sold									
Gross profit									
Gross margin									
By product model for each product									

Format 4

Market Share Assessment Relative to the Market ($ thousands)

Last Three Years

	19 ___ Units	Rate of Growth (%)	19 ___ Units	Rate of Growth (%)	19 ___ Units	Rate of Growth (%)
Market share (Units)						
Market share (Relative to market)						
Overall:						
Product:						
Product:						
Product:						
Product:						
Product:						
Product:						
Product:						
Product:						
Product:						
Product:						
Product:						
Product:						

Format 4 (Continued)

Market Share Assessment Relative to the Market ($ thousands)

Next Three Years

	19 ___ Units	Rate of Growth (%)	19 ___ Units	Rate of Growth (%)	19 ___ Units	Rate of Growth (%)
Market share (Units)						
Market share (Relative to market)						
Overall:						
Product:						
Product:						
Product:						
Product:						
Product:						
Product:						
Product:						
Product:						
Product:						
Product:						
Product:						
Product:						

Format 5

Market Share Assessment Relative to the Competition ($ thousands)

Last Three Years

	19 ___ Units	Rate of Growth (%)	19 ___ Units	Rate of Growth (%)	19 ___ Units	Rate of Growth (%)

Market share (Relative to competition)

Overall:

Product:

Product:

Product:

Product:

Product:

Product:

Product:

Product:

Product:

Product:

Product:

Format 5 (Continued)

Market Share Assessment Relative to the Competition ($ thousands)

Next Three Years

	19 ___ Units	Rate of Growth (%)	19 ___ Units	Rate of Growth (%)	19 ___ Units	Rate of Growth (%)

Market share (Relative to competition)

Overall:

Product:

Product:

Product:

Product:

Product:

Product:

Product:

Product:

Product:

Product:

Product:

Product:

Format 6

Target Market/Customer Identification

Target Market

1		2	
Descriptors	**Counts**	**Descriptors**	**Counts**
a.			
b.			
c.			

Total*

* Total represents cross-tabulation among descriptors, not total counts of descriptors.

Format 7

Product Positioning Attributes

Last Year

	Attributes		Products	
	A:		A:	1:
	B:		B:	2:
	C:			
	D:			

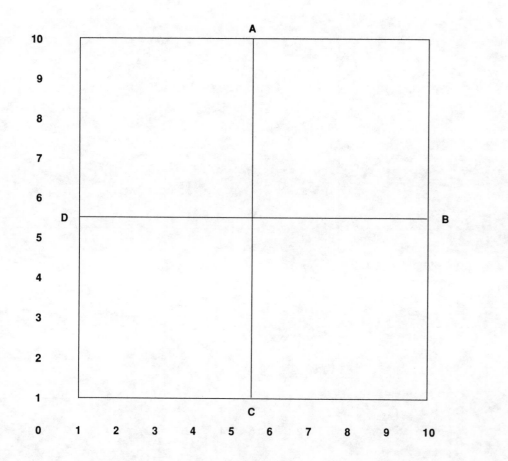

Format 7 (Continued)

Product Positioning Attributes

Next Year

Attributes		Products	
A:		A:	1:
B:		B:	2:
C:			
D:			

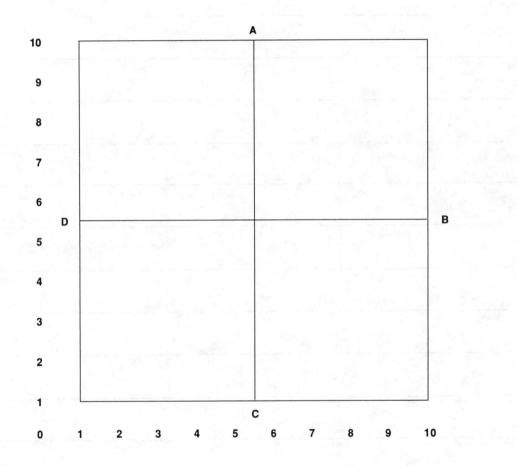

Format 8

Format 8 (Continued)

Penetration Strategy Assessment

Last Year

By Product	Short-Term Commitment	Long-Term Commitment

By Overall Product Line

Format 8 (Continued)

Penetration Strategy Assessment

Next Year

By Product	Short-Term Commitment	Long-Term Commitment

By Overall Product Line

Marketing Function Activities

Formats 9–65 should be used to help you identify the marketing mix components used to get your products or services to the marketplace. See Unit 2 in Part 1 for explanations and examples of the formats.

Format 9

Marketing Research Budget

Last Three Years

Activity	19 __ Costs ($)	Percentage of Sales	19 __ Costs ($)	Percentage of Sales	19 __ Costs ($)	Percentage of Sales
Total						

Next Three Years

Activity	19 __ Costs ($)	Percentage of Sales	19 __ Costs ($)	Percentage of Sales	19 __ Costs ($)	Percentage of Sales
Total						

Format 10

Types of Research Performed

Last Three Years

By Product	Types of Research Performed	Results

By Overall Product Line

By Product	Types of Research Performed	Results

By Overall Product Line

By Product	Types of Research Performed	Results

By Overall Product Line

Format 10 (Continued)

Types of Research Performed

Next Three Years

By Product	Types of Research Performed	Results

By Overall Product Line

By Product	Types of Research Performed	Results

By Overall Product Line

By Product	Types of Research Performed	Results

By Overall Product Line

Format 11

Types of Research Techniques Used

Last Three Years

By Product	Types of Research Techniques Used	Results

By Overall Product Line

By Product	Types of Research Techniques Used	Results

By Overall Product Line

By Product	Types of Research Techniques Used	Results

By Overall Product Line

Format 11 (Continued)

Types of Research Techniques Used

Next Three Years

By Product	Types of Research Techniques Used	Results

By Overall Product Line

By Product	Types of Research Techniques Used	Results

By Overall Product Line

By Product	Types of Research Techniques Used	Results

By Overall Product Line

Format 12

Types of Research Methods Used

Last Three Years

19 ___

By Product	Types of Research Methods Used	Results

By Overall Product Line

19 ___

By Product	Types of Research Methods Used	Results

By Overall Product Line

19 ___

By Product	Types of Research Methods Used	Results

By Overall Product Line

Format 12 (Continued)

Types of Research Methods Used

Next Three Years

By Product   19 ___   Types of Research Methods Used   Results

By Overall Product Line

By Product   19 ___   Types of Research Methods Used   Results

By Overall Product Line

By Product   19 ___   Types of Research Methods Used   Results

By Overall Product Line

Format 13

Types of Research Instruments Used

Last Three Years

By Product

19 ___
Types of Research Instruments Used

Results

By Overall Product Line

By Product

19 ___
Types of Research Instruments Used

Results

By Overall Product Line

By Product

19 ___
Types of Research Instruments Used

Results

By Overall Product Line

Format 13 (Continued)

Types of Research Instruments Used

Next Three Years

By Product   19 ___
                          Types of Research Instruments Used   **Results**

By Overall Product Line

By Product   19 ___
                          Types of Research Instruments Used   **Results**

By Overall Product Line

By Product   19 ___
                          Types of Research Instruments Used   **Results**

By Overall Product Line

Format 14

Types of Tabulation and Analysis Used

Last Three Years

By Product	19 ___ Types of Tabulation and Analysis Used	Results

By Overall Product Line

By Product	19 ___ Types of Tabulation and Analysis Used	Results

By Overall Product Line

By Product	19 ___ Types of Tabulation and Analysis Used	Results

By Overall Product Line

102

Format 14 (Continued)

Types of Tabulation and Analysis Used

Next Three Years

By Product	19 ___ Types of Tabulation and Analysis Used	Results

By Overall Product Line

By Product	19 ___ Types of Tabulation and Analysis Used	Results

By Overall Product Line

By Product	19 ___ Types of Tabulation and Analysis Used	Results

By Overall Product Line

Format 15

Changes Made to Marketing Plans

Last Three Years

By Product	19 ___ Effect on Marketing Plans	Results

_____

_____

_____

By Overall Product Line

===

By Product	19 ___ Effect on Marketing Plans	Results

_____

_____

_____

By Overall Product Line

===

By Product	19 ___ Effect on Marketing Plans	Results

_____

_____

_____

By Overall Product Line

===

Format 15 (Continued)

Changes Made to Marketing Plans

Next Three Years

By Product	19 ___ Effect on Marketing Plans	Results

By Overall Product Line

By Product	19 ___ Effect on Marketing Plans	Results

By Overall Product Line

By Product	19 ___ Effect on Marketing Plans	Results

By Overall Product Line

Format 16

Product Development Budget

Last Three Years

Activity	19 ___ Costs ($)	Percentage of Sales	19 ___ Costs ($)	Percentage of Sales	19 ___ Costs ($)	Percentage of Sales
Total						

Next Three Years

Activity	19 ___ Costs ($)	Percentage of Sales	19 ___ Costs ($)	Percentage of Sales	19 ___ Costs ($)	Percentage of Sales
Total						

Format 17

Existing Product Line Strategy

Last Three Years

By Product	Existing Product Line Strategies	Results

By Overall Product Line

By Product	Existing Product Line Strategies	Results

By Overall Product Line

By Product	Existing Product Line Strategies	Results

By Overall Product Line

Format 17 (Continued)

Existing Product Line Strategy

Next Three Years

By Product	Existing Product Line Strategies	Results

By Overall Product Line

By Product	Existing Product Line Strategies	Results

By Overall Product Line

By Product	Existing Product Line Strategies	Results

By Overall Product Line

Format 18

Format 18 (Continued)

New Product Line Strategy

Last Three Years

By Product	New Product Line Strategies	Results

By Overall Product Line

By Product	New Product Line Strategies	Results

By Overall Product Line

By Product	New Product Line Strategies	Results

By Overall Product Line

109

Format 18 (Continued)

New Product Line Strategy

Next Three Years

By Product	New Product Line Strategies	Results

By Overall Product Line

By Product	New Product Line Strategies	Results

By Overall Product Line

By Product	New Product Line Strategies	Results

By Overall Product Line

Format 19

Product Mix Modification Strategy

Last Three Years

By Product	Product Mix Modification Strategies	Results

By Overall Product Line

By Product	Product Mix Modification Strategies	Results

By Overall Product Line

By Product	Product Mix Modification Strategies	Results

By Overall Product Line

Format 19 (Continued)

Product Mix Modification Strategy

Next Three Years

By Product	Product Mix Modification Strategies	Results

By Overall Product Line

By Product	Product Mix Modification Strategies	Results

By Overall Product Line

By Product	Product Mix Modification Strategies	Results

By Overall Product Line

Format 20

Branding Strategies

Last Three Years

By Product	Branding Strategies	Results

By Overall Product Line

By Product	Branding Strategies	Results

By Overall Product Line

By Product	Branding Strategies	Results

By Overall Product Line

Format 20 (Continued)

Branding Strategies

Next Three Years

By Product	Branding Strategies	Results

By Overall Product Line

By Product	Branding Strategies	Results

By Overall Product Line

By Product	Branding Strategies	Results

By Overall Product Line

Format 21

Packaging Strategies

Last Three Years

By Product	Packaging Strategies	Results

By Overall Product Line

By Product	Packaging Strategies	Results

By Overall Product Line

By Product	Packaging Strategies	Results

By Overall Product Line

Format 21 (Continued)

Packaging Strategies

Next Three Years

By Product	Packaging Strategies	Results

By Overall Product Line

By Product	Packaging Strategies	Results

By Overall Product Line

By Product	Packaging Strategies	Results

By Overall Product Line

116

Format 22

Service Enhancements

Last Three Years

By Product	Service Enhancements	Results

By Overall Product Line

By Product	Service Enhancements	Results

By Overall Product Line

By Product	Service Enhancements	Results

By Overall Product Line

Format 22 (Continued)

Service Enhancements

Next Three Years

By Product	Service Enhancements	Results

By Overall Product Line

By Product	Service Enhancements	Results

By Overall Product Line

By Product	Service Enhancements	Results

By Overall Product Line

Format 23

Pricing Budget

Last Three Years

Activity	19 ___ Costs ($)	Percentage of Sales	19 ___ Costs ($)	Percentage of Sales	19 ___ Costs ($)	Percentage of Sales
Total						

Next Three Years

Activity	19 ___ Costs ($)	Percentage of Sales	19 ___ Costs ($)	Percentage of Sales	19 ___ Costs ($)	Percentage of Sales
Total						

119

Format 24

Pricing Formula Criteria

Last Three Years

By Product (per unit)	Base	Range	Maximum	19____

By Overall Product Line

By Product (per unit)	Base	Range	Maximum	19____

By Overall Product Line

By Product (per unit)	Base	Range	Maximum	19____

By Overall Product Line

120

Format 24 (Continued)

Pricing Formula Criteria

Next Three Years

By Product (per unit)	Base	Range	Maximum	19____

By Overall Product Line

By Product (per unit)	Base	Range	Maximum	19____

By Overall Product Line

By Product (per unit)	Base	Range	Maximum	19____

By Overall Product Line

Format 25

Price Strategies

Last Three Years

By Product   **Pricing Strategies**   **19___**

By Overall Product Line

By Product   **Pricing Strategies**   **19___**

By Overall Product Line

By Product   **Pricing Strategies**   **19___**

By Overall Product Line

Format 25 (Continued)

Price Strategies

Next Three Years

By Product	Pricing Strategies	19____

By Overall Product Line

By Product	Pricing Strategies	19____

By Overall Product Line

By Product	Pricing Strategies	19____

By Overall Product Line

Format 26

Format 26 (Continued)

Price/Cost Structure

Last Three Years

19___   Product : _____   Product: _____

Volume (Units)   1–   1–
_____

Price ($)
_____

Discount ($)
_____

Revenue ($)
_____

Gross costs ($)
_____

Gross profit ($)
_____

Gross margin (%)
_____

19___   Product : _____   Product: _____

Volume (Units)   1–   1–
_____

Price ($)
_____

Discount ($)
_____

Revenue ($)
_____

Gross costs ($)
_____

Gross profit ($)
_____

Gross margin (%)
_____

19___   Product : _____   Product: _____

Volume (Units)   1–   1–
_____

Price ($)
_____

Discount ($)
_____

Revenue ($)
_____

Gross costs ($)
_____

Gross profit ($)
_____

Gross margin (%)
_____

Format 26 (Continued)

Price/Cost Structure

Next Three Years

19____

Volume (Units)	Product :			Product:		
	1–5	6–10	11+	1–5	6–10	11+
Price ($)						
Discount ($)						
Revenue ($)						
Gross costs ($)						
Gross profit ($)						
Gross margin (%)						

19____

Volume (Units)	Product :			Product:		
	1–5	6–10	11+	1–5	6–10	11+
Price ($)						
Discount ($)						
Revenue ($)						
Gross costs ($)						
Gross profit ($)						
Gross margin (%)						

19____

Volume (Units)	Product :			Product:		
	1–5	6–10	11+	1–5	6–10	11+
Price ($)						
Discount ($)						
Revenue ($)						
Gross costs ($)						
Gross profit ($)						
Gross margin (%)						

Format 27

Distribution Budget

Last Three Years

Activity	19 ___ Costs ($)	Percentage of Sales	19 ___ Costs ($)	Percentage of Sales	19 ___ Costs ($)	Percentage of Sales
Total						

Next Three Years

Activity	19 ___ Costs ($)	Percentage of Sales	19 ___ Costs ($)	Percentage of Sales	19 ___ Costs ($)	Percentage of Sales
Total						

Format 28

Format 28 (Continued)

Channel Selections

Last Three Years

By Product   **Channel Selections**   **19**___

_____

_____

_____

_____

By Overall Product Line

===

By Product   **Channel Selections**   **19**___

_____

_____

_____

_____

By Overall Product Line

===

By Product   **Channel Selections**   **19**___

_____

_____

_____

_____

By Overall Product Line

===

Format 28 (Continued)

Channel Selections

Next Three Years

By Product   **Channel Selections**   **19**_____

By Overall Product Line

By Product   **Channel Selections**   **19**_____

By Overall Product Line

By Product   **Channel Selections**   **19**_____

By Overall Product Line

Format 29

Distribution Strategies

Last Three Years

By Product　　　　　　　　　**Distribution Strategies**　　　　　　　　　**19____**

_____

_____

_____

_____

By Overall Product Line

===

By Product　　　　　　　　　**Distribution Strategies**　　　　　　　　　**19____**

_____

_____

_____

_____

By Overall Product Line

===

By Product　　　　　　　　　**Distribution Strategies**　　　　　　　　　**19____**

_____

_____

_____

_____

By Overall Product Line

===

129

Format 29 (Continued)

Distribution Strategies

Next Three Years

By Product   **Distribution Strategies**   **19**____

By Overall Product Line

By Product   **Distribution Strategies**   **19**____

By Overall Product Line

By Product   **Distribution Strategies**   **19**____

By Overall Product Line

Format 30

Contracts Awarded and Status

Last Three Years

By Product   **Contracts Awarded**   **19____**

_____

_____

_____

_____

_____

By Overall Product Line

_____

By Product   **Contracts Awarded**   **19____**

_____

_____

_____

_____

By Overall Product Line

_____

By Product   **Contracts Awarded**   **19____**

_____

_____

_____

_____

By Overall Product Line

_____

Format 30 (Continued)

Contracts Awarded and Status

Next Three Years

By Product	Contracts Awarded	19___

By Overall Product Line

By Product	Contracts Awarded	19___

By Overall Product Line

By Product	Contracts Awarded	19___

By Overall Product Line

Format 31

Sales Management Budget

Last Three Years

Activity	19 ___ Costs ($)	Percentage of Sales	19 ___ Costs ($)	Percentage of Sales	19 ___ Costs ($)	Percentage of Sales
Total*						

*Total budget does *not* include salesperson's compensation.

Next Three Years

Activity	19 ___ Costs ($)	Percentage of Sales	19 ___ Costs ($)	Percentage of Sales	19 ___ Costs ($)	Percentage of Sales
Total*						

*Total budget does *not* include salesperson's compensation.

133

Format 32

Sales Force Activities

Last Three Years

By Product　　　　　　　　　　　**Sales Force**　　　　　　　　　　　　　　　　　　　　**19____**

_____

_____

_____

_____

By Overall Product Line

===

By Product　　　　　　　　　　　**Sales Force**　　　　　　　　　　　　　　　　　　　　**19____**

_____

_____

_____

_____

By Overall Product Line

===

By Product　　　　　　　　　　　**Sales Force**　　　　　　　　　　　　　　　　　　　　**19____**

_____

_____

_____

_____

By Overall Product Line

===

Format 32 (Continued)

Sales Force Activities

Next Three Years

By Product	Sales Force	19___

By Overall Product Line

By Product	Sales Force	19___

By Overall Product Line

By Product	Sales Force	19___

By Overall Product Line

Format 33

Format 33 (Continued)

Internal Sales Promotions

Last Three Years

By Product   **Sales Promotions**   **19** ____

By Overall Product Line

By Product   **Sales Promotions**   **19** ____

By Overall Product Line

By Product   **Sales Promotions**   **19** ____

By Overall Product Line

Format 33 (Continued)

Internal Sales Promotions

Next Three Years

By Product	**Sales Promotions**	**19**

By Overall Product Line

By Product	**Sales Promotions**	**19**

By Overall Product Line

By Product	**Sales Promotions**	**19**

By Overall Product Line

Format 34

Format 34 (Continued)

Sales Quota and Compensation Plans

Last Three Years

Salesperson	19 ___		19 ___		Rate of Growth (%)	19 ___		Rate of Growth (%)
	$	Units	$	Units		$	Units	
Total								

Format 34 (Continued)

Salesperson ——————————————

| **By Product** | **Compensation Programs** | **19** —— |

———————————————————————————————

———————————————————————————————

———————————————————————————————

———————————————————————————————

By Overall Product Line

═══════════════════════════════

| **By Product** | **Compensation Programs** | **19** —— |

———————————————————————————————

———————————————————————————————

———————————————————————————————

———————————————————————————————

By Overall Product Line

═══════════════════════════════

| **By Product** | **Compensation Programs** | **19** —— |

———————————————————————————————

———————————————————————————————

———————————————————————————————

———————————————————————————————

By Overall Product Line

═══════════════════════════════

Format 34 (Continued)

Sales and Compensation Plans

Next Three Years

Salesperson	19 ___ $	Units	19 ___ $	Units	Rate of Growth (%)	19 ___ $	Units	Rate of Growth (%)
Total								

Format 34 (Continued)

Salesperson —————————————

By Product   **Compensation Programs**   **19** ——

By Overall Product Line

===

By Product   **Compensation Programs**   **19** ——

By Overall Product Line

===

By Product   **Compensation Programs**   **19** ——

By Overall Product Line

===

Format 35

Prospecting Methods

Last Three Years

By Product	Prospecting Methods	19___

By Overall Product Line

By Product	Prospecting Methods	19___

By Overall Product Line

By Product	Prospecting Methods	19___

By Overall Product Line

Format 35 (Continued)

Prospecting Methods

Next Three Years

By Product   **Prospecting Methods**   **19____**

_____

_____

_____

_____

_____

By Overall Product Line

===

By Product   **Prospecting Methods**   **19____**

_____

_____

_____

_____

By Overall Product Line

===

By Product   **Prospecting Methods**   **19____**

_____

_____

_____

_____

By Overall Product Line

===

Format 36

Territory Control Definition

Last Three Years

By Product	Territory Assignment	Salesperson Assignment	19___

_____

_____

_____

_____

By Overall Product Line

By Product	Territory Assignment	Salesperson Assignment	19___

_____

_____

_____

_____

By Overall Product Line

By Product	Territory Assignment	Salesperson Assignment	19___

_____

_____

_____

_____

By Overall Product Line

Format 36 (Continued)

Territory Control Definition

Next Three Years

By Product	Territory Assignment	Salesperson Assignment	19____

By Overall Product Line

By Product	Territory Assignment	Salesperson Assignment	19____

By Overall Product Line

By Product	Territory Assignment	Salesperson Assignment	19____

By Overall Product Line

Format 37

Sales Activity Tracking

Last Three Years

By Product   **Sales Activity**   **19**___

_____

_____

_____

_____

By Overall Product Line

═══

By Product   **Sales Activity**   **19**___

_____

_____

_____

_____

By Overall Product Line

═══

By Product   **Sales Activity**   **19**___

_____

_____

_____

_____

By Overall Product Line

═══

Format 37 (Continued)

Sales Activity Tracking

Next Three Years

By Product	Sales Activity	19____

By Overall Product Line

By Product	Sales Activity	19____

By Overall Product Line

By Product	Sales Activity	19____

By Overall Product Line

Format 38

Advertising Budget

Last Three Years

Activity	19 ___ Costs ($)	Percentage of Sales	19 ___ Costs ($)	Percentage of Sales	19 ___ Costs ($)	Percentage of Sales
Total						

Next Three Years

Activity	19 ___ Costs ($)	Percentage of Sales	19 ___ Costs ($)	Percentage of Sales	19 ___ Costs ($)	Percentage of Sales
Total						

Format 39

Message/Theme Strategies for Advertising

Last Three Years

By Product	Message/Theme Used	19 ____

By Overall Product Line

By Product	Message/Theme Used	19 ____

By Overall Product Line

By Product	Message/Theme Used	19 ____

By Overall Product Line

Format 39 (Continued)

Message/Theme Strategies for Advertising

Next Three Years

By Product	Messages/Themes Used	19 ___

By Overall Product Line

By Product	Messages/Themes Used	19 ___

By Overall Product Line

By Product	Messages/Themes Used	19 ___

By Overall Product Line

Format 40

Creative Developments for Advertising

Last Three Years

By Product	Creative Developments	19 ___

By Overall Product Line

By Product	Creative Developments	19 ___

By Overall Product Line

By Product	Creative Developments	19 ___

By Overall Product Line

151

Format 40 (Continued)

Creative Developments for Advertising

Next Three Years

By Product	Creative Developments	**19** ___

_____

_____

_____

_____

By Overall Product Line

═══

By Product	Creative Developments	**19** ___

_____

_____

_____

_____

By Overall Product Line

═══

By Product	Creative Developments	**19** ___

_____

_____

_____

_____

By Overall Product Line

═══

Format 41

Final Production Management for Advertising

Last Three Years

By Product   **Production Management**   **19** ____

_____

_____

_____

_____

_____

By Overall Product Line

===

By Product   **Production Management**   **19** ____

_____

_____

_____

_____

_____

By Overall Product Line

===

By Product   **Production Management**   **19** ____

_____

_____

_____

_____

_____

By Overall Product Line

===

Format 41 (Continued)

Final Production Management for Advertising

Next Three Years

By Product   **Production Management**   **19** ___

By Overall Product Line

By Product   **Production Management**   **19** ___

By Overall Product Line

By Product   **Production Management**   **19** ___

By Overall Product Line

Format 42

Format 42 (Continued)

Legal Ramifications of Advertising Content

Last Three Years

By Product	Legal Ramifications		19 ___

By Overall Product Line

By Product	Legal Ramifications		19 ___

By Overall Product Line

By Product	Legal Ramifications		19 ___

By Overall Product Line

Format 42 (Continued)

Legal Ramifications of Advertising Content

Next Three Years

By Product	Legal Ramifications	19 ___

By Overall Product Line

By Product	Legal Ramifications	19 ___

By Overall Product Line

By Product	Legal Ramifications	19 ___

By Overall Product Line

Format 43

Media Strategies for Advertising

Last Three Years

By Product	Media Strategies	19 ___

By Overall Product Line

By Product	Media Strategies	19 ___

By Overall Product Line

By Product	Media Strategies	19 ___

By Overall Product Line

Format 43 (Continued)

Media Strategies for Advertising

Next Three Years

By Product	Media Strategies	19 ___

By Overall Product Line

By Product	Media Strategies	19 ___

By Overall Product Line

By Product	Media Strategies	19 ___

By Overall Product Line

Format 44

Format 43 (Continued)

Media Selections for Advertising

Last Three Years

By Product   **Mediums Used**   **19** ___

_____

_____

_____

_____

_____

By Overall Product Line

===

By Product   **Mediums Used**   **19** ___

_____

_____

_____

_____

By Overall Product Line

===

By Product   **Mediums Used**   **19** ___

_____

_____

_____

_____

By Overall Product Line

===

Format 44 (Continued)

Media Selections for Advertising

Next Three Years

By Product	Mediums Used	19 ___

By Overall Product Line

By Product	Mediums Used	19 ___

By Overall Product Line

By Product	Mediums Used	19 ___

By Overall Product Line

Format 45

Advertising Response Tracking Results

Last Three Years

By Product	Advertising Response Tracking	19 ____

By Overall Product Line

By Product	Advertising Response Tracking	19 ____

By Overall Product Line

By Product	Advertising Response Tracking	19 ____

By Overall Product Line

161

Format 45 (Continued)

Advertising Response Tracking Results

Next Three Years

By Product	Advertising Response Tracking	19 ____

_____

_____

_____

_____

By Overall Product Line

_____
_____

By Product	Advertising Response Tracking	19 ____

_____

_____

_____

_____

By Overall Product Line

_____
_____

By Product	Advertising Response Tracking	19 ____

_____

_____

_____

_____

By Overall Product Line

_____
_____

Format 46

Promotion Budget

Last Three Years

Activity	19 ___ Costs ($)	Percentage of Sales	19 ___ Costs ($)	Percentage of Sales	19 ___ Costs ($)	Percentage of Sales
Total						

Next Three Years

Activity	19 ___ Costs ($)	Percentage of Sales	19 ___ Costs ($)	Percentage of Sales	19 ___ Costs ($)	Percentage of Sales
Total						

Format 47

Message/Theme Strategies for Promotion Activities

Last Three Years

By Product   **Message/Theme Used**   **19 ___**

_____

_____

_____

_____

By Overall Product Line

==

By Product   **Message/Theme Used**   **19 ___**

_____

_____

_____

_____

By Overall Product Line

==

By Product   **Message/Theme Used**   **19 ___**

_____

_____

_____

_____

By Overall Product Line

==

Format 47 (Continued)

Message/Theme Strategies for Promotion Activities

Next Three Years

By Product	Message/Theme Used	19 ___

By Overall Product Line

By Product	Message/Theme Used	19 ___

By Overall Product Line

By Product	Message/Theme Used	19 ___

By Overall Product Line

Format 48

Creative Developments for Promotion Activities

Last Three Years

By Product	Creative Developments	19 ___

By Overall Product Line

By Product	Creative Developments	19 ___

By Overall Product Line

By Product	Creative Developments	19 ___

By Overall Product Line

Format 48 (Continued)

Creative Developments for Promotion Activities

Next Three Years

By Product	Creative Developments	19 ___

By Overall Product Line

By Product	Creative Developments	19 ___

By Overall Product Line

By Product	Creative Developments	19 ___

By Overall Product Line

Format 49

Final Production Management for Promotion Activities

Last Three Years

By Product   **Production Management**   **19** ____

_____

_____

_____

_____

By Overall Product Line

===

By Product   **Production Management**   **19** ____

_____

_____

_____

_____

By Overall Product Line

===

By Product   **Production Management**   **19** ____

_____

_____

_____

_____

By Overall Product Line

===

Format 49 (Continued)

Final Production Management for Promotion Activities

Next Three Years

By Product   **Production Management**   **19** ____

By Overall Product Line

By Product   **Production Management**   **19** ____

By Overall Product Line

By Product   **Production Management**   **19** ____

By Overall Product Line

Format 50

Legal Ramifications of Promotion Activities

Last Three Years

By Product	Legal Ramifications	19 ___

By Overall Product Line

By Product	Legal Ramifications	19 ___

By Overall Product Line

By Product	Legal Ramifications	19 ___

By Overall Product Line

170

Format 50 (Continued)

Legal Ramifications of Promotion Activities

Next Three Years

By Product	Legal Ramifications	19 ___

By Overall Product Line

By Product	Legal Ramifications	19 ___

By Overall Product Line

By Product	PLegal Ramifications	19 ___

By Overall Product Line

Format 51

Media Strategies for Promotion Activities

Last Three Years

By Product	Media Strategies	19 ____

By Overall Product Line

By Product	Media Strategies	19 ____

By Overall Product Line

By Product	Media Strategies	19 ____

By Overall Product Line

172

Format 51 (Continued)

Media Strategies for Promotion Activities

Next Three Years

By Product   **Media Strategies**   **19** ____

_____

_____

_____

_____

By Overall Product Line

═══

By Product   **Media Strategies**   **19** ____

_____

_____

_____

_____

By Overall Product Line

═══

By Product   **Media Strategies**   **19** ____

_____

_____

_____

_____

By Overall Product Line

═══

Format 52

Media Selections for Promotion Activities

Last Three Years

By Product	Medium Used	19 ____

By Overall Product Line

By Product	Medium Used	19 ____

By Overall Product Line

By Product	Medium Used	19 ____

By Overall Product Line

174

Format 52 (Continued)

Media Selections for Promotion Activities

Next Three Years

By Product	Medium Used	19____

By Overall Product Line

By Product	Medium Used	19____

By Overall Product Line

By Product	Medium Used	19____

By Overall Product Line

Format 53

Format 53 (Continued)

Promotions Response Tracking Results

Last Three Years

By Product   **Promotions Response Tracking**   **19** ___

_____

_____

_____

_____

By Overall Product Line

===

By Product   **Promotions Response Tracking**   **19** ___

_____

_____

_____

_____

By Overall Product Line

===

By Product   **Promotions Response Tracking**   **19** ___

_____

_____

_____

_____

By Overall Product Line

===

Format 53 (Continued)

Promotions Response Tracking Results

Next Three Years

By Product   **Promotions Response Tracking**   **19 ____**

By Overall Product Line

By Product   **Promotions Response Tracking**   **19 ____**

By Overall Product Line

By Product   **Promotions Response Tracking**   **19 ____**

By Overall Product Line

Format 54

Public Relations Budget

Last Three Years

Activity	19 ___ Costs ($)	Percentage of Sales	19 ___ Costs ($)	Percentage of Sales	19 ___ Costs ($)	Percentage of Sales
Total						

Next Three Years

Activity	19 ___ Costs ($)	Percentage of Sales	19 ___ Costs ($)	Percentage of Sales	19 ___ Costs ($)	Percentage of Sales
Total						

Format 55

Message/Theme Strategies for Public Relations

Last Three Years

By Product	Message/Theme Used	19 ___

By Overall Product Line

By Product	Message/Theme Used	19 ___

By Overall Product Line

By Product	Message/Theme Used	19 ___

By Overall Product Line

Format 55 (Continued)

Message/Theme Strategies for Public Relations

Next Three Years

By Product	Message/Theme Used	19 ___

_____

_____

_____

_____

By Overall Product Line

══

By Product	Message/Theme Used	19 ___

_____

_____

_____

By Overall Product Line

══

By Product	Message/Theme Used	19 ___

_____

_____

_____

_____

By Overall Product Line

══

Format 56

Creative Developments for Public Relations

Last Three Years

By Product	**Creative Developments**	**19** __

_____

_____

_____

_____

_____

By Overall Product Line

==

By Product	**Creative Developments**	**19** __

_____

_____

_____

_____

By Overall Product Line

==

By Product	**Creative Developments**	**19** __

_____

_____

_____

_____

By Overall Product Line

==

Format 56 (Continued)

Creative Developments for Public Relations

Next Three Years

By Product	Creative Developments	19 ___

By Overall Product Line

By Product	Creative Developments	19 ___

By Overall Product Line

By Product	Creative Developments	19 ___

By Overall Product Line

Format 57

Final Production Management for Public Relations

Last Three Years

By Product   **Production Management**   **19 _____**

By Overall Product Line

===

By Product   **Production Management**   **19 _____**

By Overall Product Line

===

By Product   **Production Management**   **19 _____**

By Overall Product Line

===

Format 57 (Continued)

Final Production Management for Public Relations

Next Three Years

By Product **Production Management** **19 ___**

_____

_____

_____

_____

By Overall Product Line

===

By Product **Production Management** **19 ___**

_____

_____

_____

_____

By Overall Product Line

===

By Product **Production Management** **19 ___**

_____

_____

_____

_____

By Overall Product Line

===

Format 58

Legal Ramifications of Public Relations

Last Three Years

By Product	Legal Ramifications	19 ___

By Overall Product Line

By Product	Legal Ramifications	19 ___

By Overall Product Line

By Product	Legal Ramifications	19 ___

By Overall Product Line

Format 58 (Continued)

Legal Ramifications of Public Relations

Next Three Years

By Product   **Legal Ramifications**   **19 ___**

_____

_____

_____

_____

By Overall Product Line

===

By Product   **Legal Ramifications**   **19 ___**

_____

_____

_____

_____

By Overall Product Line

===

By Product   **Legal Ramifications**   **19 ___**

_____

_____

_____

_____

By Overall Product Line

===

Format 59

Media Strategies for Public Relations

Last Three Years

By Product	Media Strategies	19 ___

By Overall Product Line

By Product	Media Strategies	19 ___

By Overall Product Line

By Product	Media Strategies	19 ___

By Overall Product Line

187

Format 59 (Continued)

Media Strategies for Public Relations

Next Three Years

By Product   **Media Strategies**   **19** ____

_____

_____

_____

_____

By Overall Product Line

==

By Product   **Media Strategies**   **19** ____

_____

_____

_____

By Overall Product Line

==

By Product   **Media Strategies**   **19** ____

_____

_____

_____

_____

By Overall Product Line

==

Format 60

Media Selections for Public Relations

Last Three Years

By Product   **Medium Used**   **19____**

_____

_____

_____

_____

By Overall Product Line

═══

By Product   **Medium Used**   **19____**

_____

_____

_____

_____

By Overall Product Line

═══

By Product   **Medium Used**   **19____**

_____

_____

_____

_____

By Overall Product Line

═══

Format 60 (Continued)

Media Selections for Public Relations

Next Three Years

By Product	Medium Used	19___

By Overall Product Line

By Product	Medium Used	19___

By Overall Product Line

By Product	Medium Used	19___

By Overall Product Line

Format 61

Format 61 (Continued)

Media Relations Practices

Last Three Years

By Product   **Media Relations**   **19** ____

_____

_____

_____

_____

By Overall Product Line

===

By Product   **Media Relations**   **19** ____

_____

_____

_____

_____

By Overall Product Line

===

By Product   **Media Relations**   **19** ____

_____

_____

_____

_____

By Overall Product Line

===

Format 61 (Continued)

Media Relations Practices

Next Three Years

By Product	Media Relations	19 ___

By Overall Product Line

By Product	Media Relations	19 ___

By Overall Product Line

By Product	Media Relations	19 ___

By Overall Product Line

Format 62

Community Involvement

Last Three Years

By Product	Community Involvement	19 ___

By Overall Product Line

By Product	Community Involvement	19 ___

By Overall Product Line

By Product	Community Involvement	19 ___

By Overall Product Line

Format 62 (Continued)

Community Involvement

Next Three Years

By Product	Community Involvement	19 ___

_____

_____

_____

_____

By Overall Product Line

By Product	Community Involvement	19 ___

_____

_____

_____

_____

By Overall Product Line

By Product	Community Involvement	19 ___

_____

_____

_____

_____

By Overall Product Line

Format 63

Public Relations Response Tracking Results

Last Three Years

By Product   **Response Tracking**   **19** ___

_____

_____

_____

_____

By Overall Product Line

===

By Product   **Response Tracking**   **19** ___

_____

_____

_____

_____

By Overall Product Line

===

By Product   **Response Tracking**   **19** ___

_____

_____

_____

_____

By Overall Product Line

===

Format 63 (Continued)

Public Relations Response Tracking Results

Next Three Years

By Product   **Response Tracking**   **19** ____

_____

_____

_____

_____

By Overall Product Line

===

By Product   **Response Tracking**   **19** ____

_____

_____

_____

_____

By Overall Product Line

===

By Product   **Response Tracking**   **19** ____

_____

_____

_____

_____

By Overall Product Line

===

Format 64

Legal Budget

Last Three Years

Activity	19 ___ Costs ($)	Percentage of Sales	19 ___ Costs ($)	Percentage of Sales	19 ___ Costs ($)	Percentage of Sales
Total						

Next Three Years

Activity	19 ___ Costs ($)	Percentage of Sales	19 ___ Costs ($)	Percentage of Sales	19 ___ Costs ($)	Percentage of Sales
Total						

Format 65

Monitoring of Legal Activities

Last Three Years

By Product   **Monitoring**   **19** ___

_____

_____

_____

_____

By Overall Product Line

═══

By Product   **Monitoring**   **19** ___

_____

_____

_____

_____

By Overall Product Line

═══

By Product   **Monitoring**   **19** ___

_____

_____

_____

_____

By Overall Product Line

═══

198

Format 65 (Continued)

Monitoring of Legal Activities

Next Three Years

By Product	Monitoring	19 ___

By Overall Product Line

By Product	Monitoring	19 ___

By Overall Product Line

By Product	Monitoring	19 ___

By Overall Product Line

Marketing Function Activities Scheduling

Formats 66–71 should be used to help you evaluate your timetable for marketing activities. In this unit, you will assess both the scheduling of your marketing functions and your media placement schedules. See Unit 3 in Part 1 for explanations and examples of the formats.

Format 66

Marketing Activities Timetable

Last Three Years

19 ____	Start/Finish (Dates)	On Time (Yes/No)	On Budget (Yes/No)	Comments

Marketing research activities:

Product development activities:

Pricing activities:

Distribution activities:

Format 66 (Continued)

Marketing Activities Timetable

Last Three Years

19 ___	Start/Finish (Dates)	On Time (Yes/No)	On Budget (Yes/No)	Comments
Sales activities:				
Advertising activities:				
Promotions activities:				
Public relations activities:				
Legal activities:				

Format 66 (Continued)

Marketing Activities Timetable

Last Three Years

19 ____	Start/Finish (Dates)	On Time (Yes/No)	On Budget (Yes/No)	Comments

Marketing research activities:

Product development activities:

Pricing activities:

Distribution activities:

Format 66 (Continued)

Marketing Activities Timetable

Last Three Years

19 ___	Start/Finish (Dates)	On Time (Yes/No)	On Budget (Yes/No)	Comments
Sales activities:				
Advertising activities:				
Promotions activities:				
Public relations activities:				
Legal activities:				

Format 66 (Continued)

Marketing Activities Timetable

Last Three Years

19 ___	Start/Finish (Dates)	On Time (Yes/No)	On Budget (Yes/No)	Comments

Marketing research activities:

Product development activities:

Pricing activities:

Distribution activities:

Format 66 (Continued)

Marketing Activities Timetable

Last Three Years

19 ____	Start/Finish (Dates)	On Time (Yes/No)	On Budget (Yes/No)	Comments
Sales activities:				
Advertising activities:				
Promotions activities:				
Public relations activities:				
Legal activities:				

Format 66 (Continued)

Marketing Activities Timetable

Next Three Years

19 ____	Start/Finish (Dates)	On Time (Yes/No)	On Budget (Yes/No)	Comments
Marketing research activities:				
Product development activities:				
Pricing activities:				
Distribution activities:				

Format 66 (Continued)

Marketing Activities Timetable

Next Three Years

19 ___	Start/Finish (Dates)	On Time (Yes/No)	On Budget (Yes/No)	Comments

Sales activities:

Advertising activities:

Promotions activities:

Public relations activities:

Legal activities:

Format 66 (Continued)

Marketing Activities Timetable

19 ___	Start/Finish (Dates)	On Time (Yes/No)	On Budget (Yes/No)	Comments

Marketing research activities:

Product development activities:

Pricing activities:

Distribution activities:

Format 66 (Continued)

Marketing Activities Timetable

Next Three Years

19 ___	Start/Finish (Dates)	On Time (Yes/No)	On Budget (Yes/No)	Comments

Sales activities:

Advertising activities:

Promotions activities:

Public relations activities:

Legal activities:

Format 66 (Continued)

Marketing Activities Timetable

Next Three Years

19 ___	Start/Finish (Dates)	On Time (Yes/No)	On Budget (Yes/No)	Comments

Marketing research activities:

Product development activities:

Pricing activities:

Distribution activities:

Format 66 (Continued)

Marketing Activities Timetable

Next Three Years

19 ___	Start/Finish (Dates)	On Time (Yes/No)	On Budget (Yes/No)	Comments
Sales activities:				
Advertising activities:				
Promotions activities:				
Public relations activities:				
Legal activities:				

Format 67

Radio Purchase Order

Client:

Product:

Message:

Date Issued:

Day	Time	Program	Seconds	From/To	Unit Cost	Frequency	Total Cost

Authorization:

Accepted by:

Format 68

Magazine Placement Schedule

Product: ___ **Begin Date:** ___ **End Date:** ___ **Date Approved:** ___ **Cost:** ___

Magazine	Jan.	Feb.	March	April	May	June	July	Aug.	Sept.	Oct.	Nov.	Dec.	Total
Name:													
Circulation:													
Closing date:	1												
Publishing frequency:	2												
Rate:	3												
Number of exposures:	4												
Contract time:	5												

Product: ___ **Begin Date:** ___ **End Date:** ___ **Date Approved:** ___ **Cost:** ___

Magazine	Jan.	Feb.	March	April	May	June	July	Aug.	Sept.	Oct.	Nov.	Dec.	Total
Name:													
Circulation:													
Closing Date:	1												
Publishing frequency:	2												
Rate:	3												
Number of Exposures:	4												
Contract time:	5												

Total ___

1: Pages
2: Ad type (purpose)
3: Color/B&W
4: Issue/Theme
5: Cost

Authorization: ___

Accepted by: ___

Format 69

Television Proposal

Product:

Message:

Date Issued:

Day	Time	Program	Seconds	Rating	HH (000)	From/To	Unit Cost	Frequency	Total Cost

Authorization:

Accepted by:

Format 70

Outdoor Proposal

Product:

Date Issued:

Position	Type	Year	Schedule	Unit Cost	No. Times	Total Cost
			Jan. Feb. March April May June July Aug. Sept. Oct. Nov. Dec.			

Authorization:

Accepted by:

Format 71

Newspaper Proposal

Newspaper:

Product:

Message:

Issued:

Day	Type/Day	Ad Size	Gross/Net	Date	Rate	Number of Inserts	Column Inches	Total Cost

Authorization:

Accepted by:

Marketing Budget

Formats 72–74 should be used to help you determine how much it has cost you to market your products and services and make sure your marketing costs are in line with national averages. See Unit 4 in Part 1 for explanations and examples of the formats.

Format 72

Individual Marketing Function's Expense Report

Last Three Years

Activity	19 ___ Costs ($)	Percentage of Sales	19 ___ Costs ($)	Percentage of Sales	19 ___ Costs ($)	Percentage of Sales
Marketing Research						
Total						
Product Development						
Total						
Pricing						
Total						
Distribution						
Total						

Format 72 (Continued)

Individual Marketing Function's Expense Report

Last Three Years

Activity	19 ___ Costs ($)	Percentage of Sales	19 ___ Costs ($)	Percentage of Sales	19 ___ Costs ($)	Percentage of Sales
Sales Management						
Total						
Advertising						
Total						
Promotions						
Total						
Public Relations						
Total						

Format 72 (Continued)

Individual Marketing Function's Expense Report

Last Three Years

Activity	19___ Costs ($)	Percentage of Sales	19___ Costs ($)	Percentage of Sales	19___ Costs ($)	Percentage of Sales
Legal						
Total						
Total						

Format 72 (Continued)

Individual Marketing Function's Expense Report

Next Three Years

Activity	19 —— Costs ($)	Percentage of Sales	19 —— Costs ($)	Percentage of Sales	19 —— Costs ($)	Percentage of Sales
Marketing Research						
Total						
Product Development						
Total						
Pricing						
Total						
Distribution						
Total						

222

Format 72 (Continued)

Individual Marketing Function's Expense Report

Next Three Years

Activity	19 ___ Costs ($)	Percentage of Sales	19 ___ Costs ($)	Percentage of Sales	19 ___ Costs ($)	Percentage of Sales
Sales Management						
Total						
Advertising						
Total						
Promotions						
Total						
Public Relations						
Total						

Format 72 (Continued)

Individual Marketing Function's Expense Report

Next Three Years

Activity	19___ Costs ($)	Percentage of Sales	19___ Costs ($)	Percentage of Sales	19___ Costs ($)	Percentage of Sales
Legal						
Total						
Total						

Format 73

Marketing Function Statement

Last Three Years

Activity	19 ___ Costs ($)	Percentage of Sales	19 ___ Costs ($)	Percentage of Sales	19 ___ Costs ($)	Percentage of Sales
Marketing Research						
Product Development						
Pricing						
Distribution						
Sales						
Advertising						
Promotion						
Public Relations						
Legal						
Total						
Percentage of Sales						
Other Marketing Expenses						
Total Marketing Budget						
Percentage of Sales						

Format 73 (Continued)

Marketing Function Statement

Next Three Years

Activity	19 ___ Costs ($)	Percentage of Sales	19 ___ Costs ($)	Percentage of Sales	19 ___ Costs ($)	Percentage of Sales
Marketing Research						
Product Development						
Pricing						
Distribution						
Sales						
Advertising						
Promotion						
Public Relations						
Legal						
Total						
Percentage of Sales						
Other Marketing Expenses						
Total Marketing Budget						
Percentage of Sales						

Format 74

Marketing Function and Product Statement

Last Three Years

19 ___

	Product: _____		Product: _____		Product: _____	
	$	%	$	%	$	%
Marketing Research						
Product Development						
Pricing						
Distribution						
Sales						
Advertising						
Promotions						
Public Relations						
Legal						
Total						
Percentage of Sales						

Format 74 (Continued)

Marketing Function and Product Statement

Last Three Years

19 ___

	Product: ___		Product: ___		Product: ___	
	$	%	$	%	$	%
Marketing Research						
Product Development						
Pricing						
Distribution						
Sales						
Advertising						
Promotions						
Public Relations						
Legal						
Total						
Percentage of Sales						

Format 74 (Continued)

Marketing Function and Product Statement

Last Three Years

19 ___

	Product:		Product:		Product:	
	$	%	$	%	$	%
Marketing Research						
Product Development						
Pricing						
Distribution						
Sales						
Advertising						
Promotions						
Public Relations						
Legal						
Total						
Percentage of Sales						

Format 74 (Continued)

Marketing Function and Product Statement

Last Three Years

19 ___

	Product:		Product:		Product:	
	$	%	$	%	$	%
Marketing Research						
Product Development						
Pricing						
Distribution						
Sales						
Advertising						
Promotions						
Public Relations						
Legal						
Total						
Percentage of Sales						

Format 74 (Continued)

Marketing Function and Product Statement

Last Three Years

19 ___

	Product:		Product:		Product:	
	$	%	$	%	$	%
Marketing Research						
Product Development						
Pricing						
Distribution						
Sales						
Advertising						
Promotions						
Public Relations						
Legal						
Total						
Percentage of Sales						

Format 74 (Continued)

Marketing Function and Product Statement

Last Three Years

19 ——

	Product:		Product:		Product:	
	$	%	$	%	$	%
Marketing Research						
Product Development						
Pricing						
Distribution						
Sales						
Advertising						
Promotions						
Public Relations						
Legal						
Total						
Percentage of Sales						

Formats for Unit 5

Marketing Control

Formats 75–77 should be used to help you measure the effectiveness of your past and present marketing control procedures. See Unit 5 in Part 1 for explanations and examples of the formats.

Format 75

Marketing Plan Reporting and Tracking

Last Three Years

Activity	Yes/No	Frequency	Results

Lead Tracking

Sales Reports Tracking

Order Taking/Processing Tracking

Next Three Years

Activity	Yes/No	Frequency	Results

Lead Tracking

Sales Reports Tracking

Order Taking/Processing Tracking

Format 76

Marketing Activity Tracking by Income Statement Analysis

Last Three Years

Item: _____	19 ___		19 ___		19 ___	
	$	Percentage	$	Percentage	$	Percentage
Gross sales						
Product A: *						
Product B: *						
Total*						
Less returns/allowances						
Net sales						
Cost of goods sold						
Beginning inventory						
Cost of goods purchased						
Total merchandise handled						
Ending inventory						
Total						
Gross profit*						
Gross profit margin*						
Marketing expenses						
Sales compensation						
Marketing functions*						
Warehousing/shipping						
Payroll taxes and insurance						
Regional office expense						
Total						
General administrative expenses						
Executive salaries						
Clerical expense						
Payroll taxes and insurance						
Office expenses						
Depreciation						
Credit/collections						
Research/development costs						
Other expenses						
Total						
Total expenses						
Net profit						

* Numbers are produced by marketing management.

Note: Percentage represents percent of sales as it relates to costs.

235

Format 76 (Continued)

Marketing Activity Tracking by Income Statement Analysis

Last Three Years

Item: _____	19 ____		19 ____		19 ____	
	$	Percentage	$	Percentage	$	Percentage
Gross sales						
Product A: *						
Product B: *						
Total*						
Less returns/allowances						
Net sales						
Cost of goods sold						
Beginning inventory						
Cost of goods purchased						
Total merchandise handled						
Ending inventory						
Total						
Gross profit*						
Gross profit margin*						
Marketing expenses						
Sales compensation						
Marketing functions*						
Warehousing/shipping						
Payroll taxes and insurance						
Regional office expense						
Total						
General administrative expenses						
Executive salaries						
Clerical expense						
Payroll taxes and insurance						
Office expenses						
Depreciation						
Credit/collections						
Research/development costs						
Other expenses						
Total						
Total expenses						
Net profit						

* Numbers are produced by marketing management.

Note: Percentage represents percent of sales as it relates to costs.

Format 77

Contingency Planning

Last Three Years

Activity	Yes/No	Frequency	Results

Marketing Research Adjustments

Contingency Planning

Next Three Years

Activity	Yes/No	Frequency	Results

Marketing Research Adjustments

Contingency Planning

About the Author

David Parmerlee is a marketing analyst and planner who works with selected clients. He is past Vice President of the Marketing Management Services Group at American Marketmetrics, Inc. A marketer with more than 12 years of experience, his approach has a financial orientation rather than the more traditional communications approach. His background is in secondary and audit research with a focus on process-based planning and implementation.

Parmerlee has worked for several major corporations, including Anheuser-Busch, Pitney Bowes, and Arthur Young (now Ernst & Young). He has represented clients in industrial, consumer, and service-based markets and has written articles for regional and national publications. He is a member of the Direct Marketing Association and the American Marketing Association, where he serves on the board of directors and the national board of standards for professional development and certification.

Parmerlee received his degrees in marketing and advertising from Ball State University in Muncie, Indiana. He is also certified as a consultant specializing in training and ethics.